TY, Thel
Films Of Thelma Ritter

Opening Credits

The film is *Rear Window*.

TY, Thel

Films Of Thelma Ritter

First edition published in Australia, May 2026.
Bent Banana Books
Lawnton, Australia, 4501.

Email bentbananabooks@gmail.com

All characters are fictitious, and any resemblance to actual persons living or dead is purely coincidental.

Cover and layout designer: Bernardos!

Cover: The cover background wash is a detail from Thel's faded floral print dress in *Pickup on South Street*.

ISBN: 978-1-7638100-7-5 Paperback

A CiP catalogue record for this book is available from the Australian National Library.

About the author

Bernie Dowling is an Australian writer working in journalism, fiction, and non-fiction.

His first novel is the neo-noir *Iraqi Icicle*. His non-fiction *Maaate! Bribe Proofing The Public Purse Against Good Blokes* is about corruption in local government.

From 2023-25, the author published a four picture-book series on film noir: *Noir Dirt Cheap*, Film *Noir Fate Vs The Working Stiff*, *Starry Starry Noir Rebels and Censors*, and *Three Faces of Noir Curse Crime Cringe*.

Man Of A Thousand Fails appeared in March 2026 and reviewed the films of legendary noir character actor, Elisha Cook Jr.

TY, Thel

Films Of Thelma Ritter

You got it mixed up with Christmas. New Year's Eve is when people go back to killing each other. – Sadie Dugan in *A Letter to Three Wives* 1949.

Thanks, Thelma, for your body of work.
May you receive a posthumous Academy
Honorary (Lifetime Achievement) Award.

Introduction

The Academy nominated which actor for best female support more times than Thelma Ritter? It is a trick question, and the answer is no one. Ritter received six nominations, one more than Amy Adams. Neither woman won an Oscar. Contrast them with the equal top male, Walter Brennan, with four nominations for best support. Brennan won three Oscars from those four nominations.

Brennan was a noir actor (*Swamp Water* 1941, *Hangmen Also Die* 1942, *To Have and Have Not* 1944, and *Nobody Lives Forever* 1946), but his wins were not for noirs. Brennan's success diverged from the results of two other noir specialists, nominated four times for best support. Between them, Arthur Kennedy and Claude Rains were eight for zero. Rains could not even take it for his great turn in *Casablanca* 1942. Charles Coburn won the 1943 Oscar for the forgotten *The More the Merrier*, an amiable unsophisticated screwball comedy, heavy on slapstick.

Supporting: Bette Davis, left, and Gene Tierney, below.

Dedicated supporter: Susan Hayward, left, Jean Peters below. Films above are *All About Eve*, left, and *The Mating Season*.

With a Song in My Heart is left and *Pickup on South Street* is below.

Day and a life sentence: Ritter's other nominations were for *Pillow Talk* 1959, with Doris Day and *Birdman of Alcatraz* 1962 with Burt Lancaster.

What Thelma said

Now I know what it feels like to be the bridesmaid and never the bride.

Ritter's remark came after her fourth unsuccessful nomination. She added an expletive or two after the sixth.

What is puzzling is that Ritter never received an Academy Honorary Award, often called a lifetime achievement award, though that can confuse it with the American Film Institute (AFI) Lifetime Achievement Award.

Ritter was 45 years old when she first appeared on the screen in the Christmas favorite *Miracle on 34th Street* 1947. Ritter plays an exhausted Every Mother admonishing Santa Claus because the store where he works has sold out the gift her son wants.

When she died in 1969, Ritter was 66 years old, significantly younger than the ages of living Academy Honorary Award holders when they received their awards. Had Ritter lived for another decade, she may have received the Academy Honorary Award.

Young at art: From left **are** honorary awardees Angela Lansbury, 88, when awarded in 2013, Myrna Loy, 85, awarded in 1991. Lillian Gish was a comparative youngster, at 77 in 1971.

Comedian Stan Laurel was an even 70 years old when he received the award in 1961. He was not in good health, and he had declined work offers after the death of his comic partner of 30 years, Oliver "Babe" Hardy, in 1957.

Screenwriter Dalton Trumbo was dead 17 years when, in 1993, he won the Best Story Oscar for *Roman Holiday* 1953. The vicious House Un-American Activities Committee blacklisted Trumbo in 1947. His Oscar was a correction of the record as British writer Ian Mclellan Hunter fronted for Trumbo on *Roman Holiday.*

Trumbo did more than the story. In 2011, the Screen Writers Guild acknowledged Trumbo as a writer of the full script. The SWG had dropped the apostrophe after writers. How standards eroded!

Earlier, in 1975, the Academy corrected the record to give Trumbo the Best Story Oscar for *The Brave One* 1956. He had used the pseudonym, Robert Rich. Trumbo's awards were corrections, not among the 29 posthumous Oscars, as of January 2026.

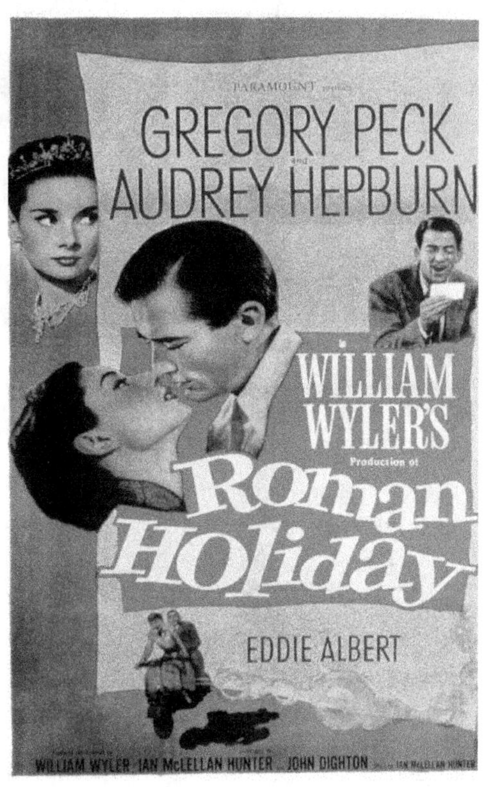

Three of the twenty-nine posthumous Oscars awarded, as of January 2026, were Academy Honorary Awards. Before I discuss the trio, I would like to record three other posthumous winners that show the diversity of such awards.

Gil Friesen was a record company executive and film producer who decided to make a great documentary about backup singers. *20 Feet from Stardom* won Best Documentary at the 86th Academy Awards in 2013, mere months after Frieson died. Eric Orbom won for Best Art Direction in 1960 for *Spartacus* 1959. He designed the good melodramas *All That Heaven Allows* 1955, and *There's Aways Tomorrow* 1955. Victor Young, the unluckiest nominee in history, won his sole award, posthumously at the 29th Academy Awards in 1957 for Best Score, for *Around the World in 80 Days*. The Academy nominated Young 22 times. If Thelma Ritter was an Academy bridesmaid, Young was a mere pageboy.

Douglas Fairbanks Sr., composer Quincy Jones, and Edward G. Robinson were the three winners of posthumous Academy Honorary Awards.

Actor Douglas Fairbanks Sr. was the first President of the Academy of Motion Picture Arts and Sciences and the first host of the Academy Awards in 1929. In 1919, Fairbanks, Mary Pickford, Charlie Chaplin and director D.W. Griffith established the film production and distribution company United Artists. He began in films as a comic and progressed to costumed adventures such as *The Mark of Zorro* 1920, *The Three Musketeers* 1921, *Robin Hood* 1922, and *Thief of Baghdad* 1924. He retired in 1934. The Academy awarded his honorary statuette in 1940, two months after his death.

Quincy Jones received seven nominations without a win, including three for the racial drama *The Color Purple* 1985, including production. Another was for the neo-noir *In Cold Blood* 1967. Neo-noirs Jones scored included *The Pawnbroker* 1964, *Mirage* 1965, *In the Heat of the Night* 1967, and *They Call Me Mr Tibbs* 1970. The Academy awarded Jones the Academy Honorary Award in March 2025, four months after his death. Talk about dying for recognition. Thelma Ritter could not achieve that.

Edward G. Robinson rose to fame in the 1930s' gangster films and continued his success with film noirs of the 1940s and 1950s. Despite his work in noir classics *Double Indemnity* 1944, *Scarlet Street* 1945, *The Red House* 1946, *Key Largo* 1948, and *House of Strangers* 1949, Robinson never received a nomination for a competitive Oscar.

The three posthumous Academy Honorary Awards were given within a year of the artists' deaths. It would be looking way back through a rear window to award Thelma, fifty-seven years after her death. Nonetheless, Ritter's film portfolio follows in the hope of such a happy ending.

– Bernie Dowling, May 2026.

Chapter 1: The Curse of the best female support Oscar

Disaster: This 2021film was a box-office bomb. Nice posters, but. Good for page 13 of this book.

Theater and movie people are superstitious. That sort of generalisation cannot be true of all movie people. But it is true enough. Of course, as a scientific cultural analyst, I do not believe in such stuff and nonsense. Sure, before I started typing on page 13, I put cloves of garlic on my desk, near the keyboard. But that is just a whim. Believers in the Curse of **Best Actress in a Supporting Role** are not whimsical.

Loyal readers know I avoid the term actress, sometimes placing me on the verge of clumsiness. The word actress is a nod to a binary definition of gender. Male actor and female actor are as well, but they mitigate against a man being billed above a woman as invariably happens in discussing awards. In the poster, right, best actor is before best actress. In this long preamble, I introduce the Curse of the Best Female Support.

OSCARS 2024 WINNERS

BEST PICTURE	BEST ACTRESS IN A LEADING ROLE	BEST ACTRESS IN A SUPPORTING ROLE
Oppenheimer (Emma Thomas, Charles Roven and Christopher Nolan, Producers)	Emma Stone (Poor Things)	Da'Vine Joy Randolph (The Holdovers)
BEST DIRECTING Christopher Nolan (Oppenheimer)		BEST WRITING (ADAPTED SCREENPLAY) American Fiction (Written for the screen by Cord Jefferson)
BEST ACTOR IN A LEADING ROLE Cillian Murphy (Oppenheimer)	BEST ACTOR IN A SUPPORTING ROLE Robert Downey Jr. (Oppenheimer)	BEST WRITING (ORIGINAL SCREENPLAY) Anatomy of a Fall (Screenplay by Justine Triet and Arthur Harari)

History does not support that a woman receiving best support will not rise to stardom. Goldie Hawn 1969, and Angelina Jolie 1999 are counterexamples. Also, established stars win best support. I will not list all, but they include noir stars Mary Astor 1941, Ethel Barrymore 1944, Claire Trevor 1948, Gloria Grahame 1952, Donna Reed 1954, Dorothy Malone 1956, Shelley Winters 1959 and 1965, and Ingrid Bergman 1974.

A curse dogged Ritter and Amy Adams with eleven noms between them for zero wins. This book is my humble attempt to help lift the curse by Thlema Ritter receiving an Academy Honorary Award. Let the campaign begin.

Chapter 2: The New Yorker

For the record: The New York State Census of 1905 records Thelma's age as three. The paper of record, the *New York Times*, has Thel's birth year wrong as 1905 in its obituary of February 3, 1969. This copy of the original is with Family Search, an online genealogical database provided as a public service by the Church of Jesus Christ of Latter-day Saints. Ring Zohran Mamdani to complain about the description of the male as head of the family.

Thelma Ritter was born in Brooklyn, New York City, in 1902, eight years before the first Hollywood movie, *In Old California* 1910, a 17-minute Western short directed by D.W. Griffith. Brooklyn had been a city of its own before 1898, when, to the chagrin of residents, it became one of the five boroughs of New York.

On a much smaller scale, a similar process happened in my area when resentment passed down the generations after North Pine District became Petrie in 1910, named after a prosperous landowner. People living in Petrie today will be nodding over their breakfast cereal at what I am recalling.

Before you jump to the conclusion that Bernie's off on another tangent, I am indicating that Brooklyn and Brooklynites have a distinctive character, independent of the rest of New York. Future character actor Ritter had a Brooklynese vernacular and a Brooklynesque style. Ritter lived in the borough of Queens from the late 1930s, but, as they say, you cannot take Brooklyn out of the girl.

Ritter's first stage role was at age 11 when she played Puck in the Junior Musical and Literary Society's *A Midsummer Night's Dream* at Montauk Theatre in Brooklyn.
Movie Pucks from left above are Mickey Rooney 1935, Ian Holm, 1968, Stanley Tucci 1999, and Avan Jogia 2017 (I know, WTP).

The theater bug had bitten Ritter. She performed in play and story readings in Brooklyn clubs and churches. She quit school to get a job and save money to enter the American Academy of Dramatic Arts. When she applied, the Academy advised Thelma to finish high school. She entered the Academy later.

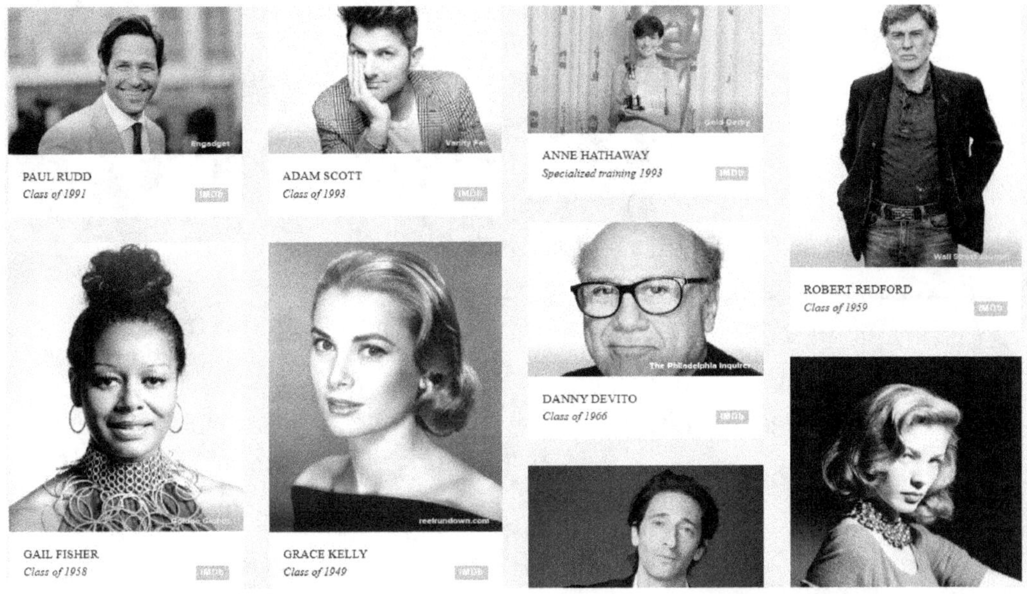

Why am I showing these pictures above? They are on page 1 of the Academy's web pages of notable students. Why is Anne Hathaway so small? "I am big," Ms. Hathaway replied. "It's the picture that's gotten small."

Thelma's picture is on there. On page 8. At least they put her there next to the Thin Man, William Powell. I hear young readers asking, "What's he talking about?" From 1934 to 1947, Myrna Loy and William Powell appeared in a series of six movies – Oh, search it.

Ritter's first gig on Broadway was in the comedy *The Shelf*, written by Dorrance Davis and produced by William B. Friedlander. The play was not a success, opening at the Morosco Theatre on September 27, 2026, and closing four days later October 1.

Playwright Davis had modest Broadway success during the 1920s. His most popular play was *Apron Strings*, which opened at the Bijou Theatre on February 17, 1930, and ran for 224 performances before closing in September 1930. Davis died on January 5, 1931, in unrecorded circumstances. He was 50 years old. Theater is a tough business.

Ritter's first Broadway play *The Shelf* at the Morosco Theatre ran for five days.

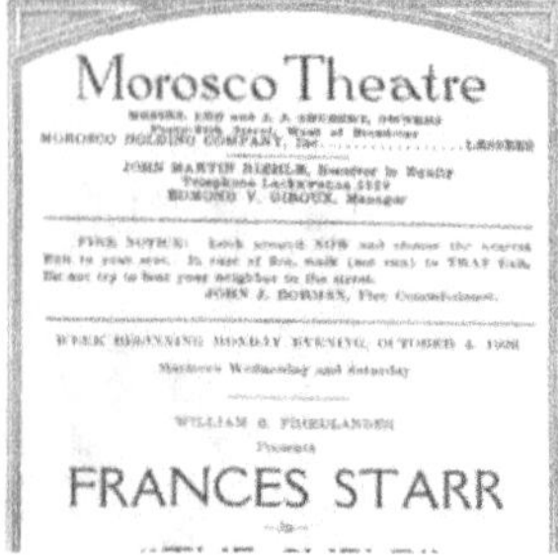

PROGRAM CONTINUED

Mrs. Chetswold	Miss Leah Winslow
Mrs. Plummer	Miss Lotta Linthicum
Miss Batterson	Miss Thelma Ritter
John Wendham	Mr. Frederick Truesdell
Caroline Wendham	Miss Lee Patrick
Stella Amaranth	MISS FRANCES STARR
Baldwin Custard	Mr. Lawrence Leslie
U. S. Senator Risdale, Stanley's father	Mr. Arthur Byron
The Rev. Herbert Chetswold	Mr. Donald Meek

PROGRAM CONTINUED ON SECOND PAGE FOLLOWING

HORTON'S ICE CREAM

1851 — The Premier Ice Cream of America For Seventy-five Years — **1926**

The Play's the thing:

After you have retrieved a tub of Horton's ice cream from the fridge and straightened your Gold Stripe stockings, let's talk about Thelma's first pro play. But first a nod to our sponsors.

In 1893, Horton sold 60 percent of ice-cream eaten by New Yorkers. The business sold in 1930, but its recipes were used up to the 1960s.

Gotham Hosiery made their first "pure silk garter-proof hose" in Jan 1911. In 1941, silk imports from Japan were banned. Nylons replaced silk.

About the play, it closed after five days. Patrick and Starr became stars of stage and screen, big and small. Patrick was Effie, Spade's secretary, in *The Maltese Falcon* 1941.

Thel, 22 years

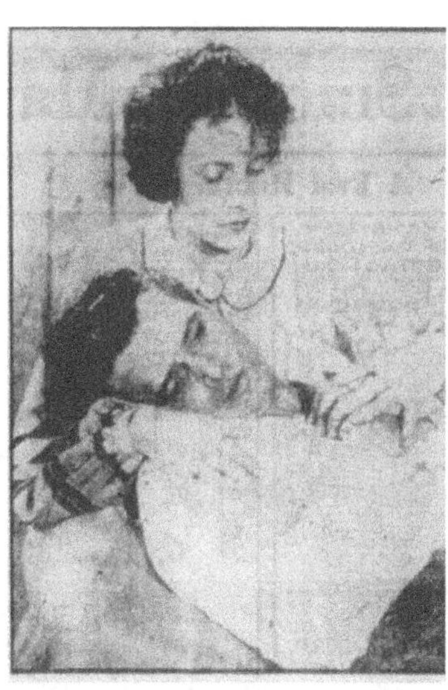

Oldies: The home of the Brooklyn Dodgers opened in 1913, the year the acting bug bit Thelma when she played Puck in *A Midsummer Night's Dream*. Ritter, above right, performed with Aldis Bartlett in the play *12 Miles Out*, a 1928 reprise of the 1925 Broadway play by William Anthony McGuire. The photo is from *The Yonkers Statesman*, Jan 7, 1928. It was Thel's last role with the Aldis Bartlett Players.

Er or Re: Theater is the common U.S. spelling, while Europe goes with theatre. U.S. playhouses, steeped in European traditions, usually call themselves theatres. Cinemas are theaters.

Doomed: Warburton alive and the Morosco, destroyed.

In 1927, Ritter performed with the fledgling theater company Aldis Bartlett Players that presented plays at Yonkers' Warburton Theatre, pictured above. The Aldis Bartlett Players bought the rights to recent Broadway hits. Thelma even played gaudy prostitute Sadie Thompson in *Rain*, a refrain of the 1922 hit by John Colton and Clemence Randolph, based on a Somerset Maugham story. Wouldn't we love a photo of that performance, but alas . . . After playing a wanton woman, she reformed in real life and married fellow actor Joseph Moran.

Buying expensive rights to recent hits and being able to afford to run them for only a week was a doomed business model. The Bartlett Players folded with debts in 1928. Urban planners demolished the Warburton building in 1974 and put up a parking lot. Despite public protests, a developer demolished the Morosco, where Thelma Ritter debuted on Broadway and which held successful award-winning plays. It was part of the Great Theater Massacre of 1982, in which five theaters died for a hotel.

By 1928, Thelma Ritter was busy playing in stock theater. Plays included a revival of the 1925 hit *Cradle Snatchers* that had Humphrey Bogart in the Broadway opening cast.

If I Was Rich reprised the 1926 Broadway play by William Anthony McGuire. Later that month in Springfield, she played a Hawaiian princess in *The Bird of Paradise* 1912 by Richard Walton Tully.

The Herald Statesman N.Y. Jan 24, 1928.

Below, The Springfield Daily Republican

Nov 04, 1928.

"If I Was Rich," at Holyoke Playhouse

Arthur Howard and Thelma Ritter, well known to Springfield theatergoers, will star in the comedy, "If I Was Rich," by William Anthony McGuire, which opens tomorrow night for a week's run at the Playhouse in Holyoke. This week Mr Howard will

Democrats Fill Warburton Theatre, At Benefit Performance Last Night— A Big Success Scored

A very enjoyable theatre party was held at the Warburton Theatre by the Al Smith for President Club of the Sixth Ward last night, the members viewing the performance of "Cradle Snatchers" which was given by the Aldis Bartlett Players.

The capacity of the theatre was taxed by the number who attended, the management of the theatre finding it necessary to open the second balcony for the first time at a benefit performance this season in order to accommodate the crowd.

In the audience were a number of the men and women prominent in Democratic politics in the city.

The performance was made particularly enjoyable by the appearance in the cast of Clara Grant Ray, wife of Charles Ray, the screen star, who took the second lead in the farce production. Between the second and third acts little Miss Bridget Mulhahey presented Miss Thelma Ritter, the leading lady, with a bouquet.

Mrs. Dennis Carroll was chairman

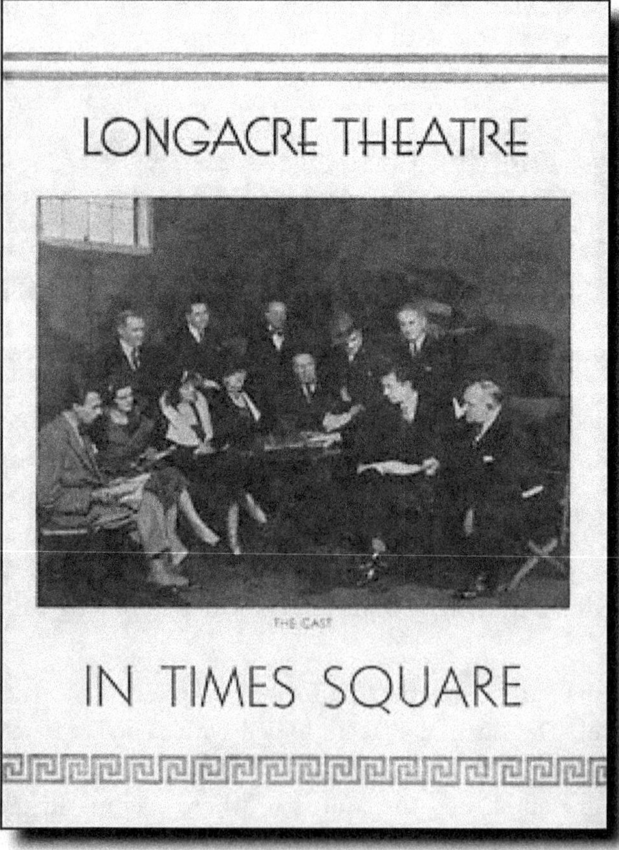

The *Daily News,* Nov 24 (page 191), derided Thelma's 1931 Broadway play *In Times Square* about play rehearsals and drug dealers. It ran for eight performances in November.

Thelma's husband, Joseph, gave up the financial uncertainty of acting and moved into advertising, which he was adept at. Ritter, too, cut back on her acting and settled into domestic life. The couple had two children, Anthony, born in 1937, and Monica, born in 1930. Both became actors, with Monica having more success.

Duet: Monica Moran, left, and Sandra Dee in *Take Her, She's Mine* 1963.

In 1966, Thelma and Monica appeared together with singer/ actor/ producer Tab Hunter in the touring musical comedy *Bye Bye Birdie*. Okay, I could not find any photos of the production, but you must admit Hunter and Divine in John Waters' 1981 satirical film *Polyester* is a good second prize.

Keep tabs on mother and daughter:

Thelma and Monica appeared with Hunter in a 1968 production of *Barefoot in the Park*. No, Thel was not Corie Bratter, the part played by Jane Fonda in the 1966 film. Monica played Corie.

After the birth of Monica, Ritter broke into radio. She guested on *The Aldrich Family* show that had a semi-permanent role for noir star and future TV witch Agnes Moorehead. Thelma was in the company of other noir stars Paul Stewart and Frank Lovejoy as guests on *Mr. District Attorney*. The Theatre of the Air reproduced successful Broadway plays. Ritter's fellow guests in the 1940s included Moorehead, Bette Davis, Katharine Hepburn, and Basil Rathbone.

Noir star: Below: Paul Stewart
Agnes Moorehead   *Walk Softly,*
The Magnificent   *Stranger* 1950
*Ambersons*1942   Right: Frank Lovejoy
The Hitch-Hiker
1953

Right: Bette Davis
The Petrified Forest
1936

Thelma Ritter might have spent the rest of her career in radio and followed the successful radio programs into television. But in the second half of the 1940s, a surprise event occurred. Some call it luck. The posh say "serendipity". We noir buffs like to think of it as Fate.

<h1 style="text-align:center">Chapter 3: Thel's movies</h1>

Spotlight on Thelma: *Pickup on South Street* 1953

I will review Ritter's film noirs, her Academy nominations, and other films that contribute to this homage or femage, which is more appropriate, despite hurting the feelings of the spellchecker.

1. *Miracle on 34th Street* 1947.
2. *Call Northside 777* 1948.
3. *A Letter to Three Wives* 1948.
4. *City Across the River* 1949.
5. *All About Eve* 1950.
6. *The Mating Season* 1950.
7. *As Young as You Feel* 1951.
8. *With a Song in My Heart* 1952.
9. *Titanic* 1953.
10. *Pickup on South Street* 1953.
11. *Rear Window* 1954.
12. *Daddy Long Legs* 1955.
13. *A Hole in the Head* 1959.
14. *Pillow Talk* 1959.
15. *The Misfits* 1961.
16. *Birdman of Alcatraz* 1962.
17. *How the West Was Won* 1962.
18. *The Incident* 1967.

Thelma Ritter was uncredited in a 1947 movie that has become a perennial Christmas favorite, *Miracle on 34th Street*. But as with successful character actors in *The Maltese Falcon* 1941 – Elisha Cook Jr., Peter Lorre and Sydney Greenstreet – it was a career-defining role for Ritter. It all began with friendship.

It sounds weird, but no woman stage-managed a Broadway production until Raymond Massey dithered across the stage as *Hamlet* in November 1931. Even weirder, Beverly Hills City Council did not have a woman councillor until 1970, nor a woman mayor until 1970. The three women were one, Phyllis Loughton, left, who became a Seaton, bottom left, through marriage.

Thelma Ritter was a neighbour and friend of Loughton before the latter moved to Hollywood to create a talent school and stock company on Paramount's lot.
– *L.A. Times* Obituary Sept. 27, 1987.

Director George Seaton filmed *Miracle on 34th Street* in New York. He invited his wife's friend radio actor Thelma to have a part. It was a tiny role, but Thel did so well, producers enlarged it to a small part. There was no credit, but audiences loved this previously unseen Everywoman.

Ritter played a working-class mom taking on department-store authority and the mighty authority of Santa Claus himself to provide her son with a Christmas present.

"Mumma wants to thank Santa Claus, too."

Thelma Ritter was 44 years old in late 1946 when the *Miracle on 34th Street* crew filmed Macy's department store's annual Thanksgiving Day Parade. The Parade has included a "welcome to Santa Claus" since its inauguration in 1924, initially as the Christmas Parade. Macy's suspended the parade during the war years 1942-44, making this year of 2026 the hundredth parade.

Thelma was 45 years old when the film launched on June 4. Hollywood is a weird town, and decided to debut the film, which became a Christmas staple on television, in early summer to attract the larger summer crowds. By sheer good luck, Fox got the best of both worlds as the movie stayed in cinemas for six months until Christmas 1947. It opened in Australia on November 21 and in the UK on December 12.

Awards

Edmund Gwenn won Best Supporting Actor. Writer/ Director George Seaton took Best Screenplay and Valentine Davies won Best Original Story. The film was nominated for Best Picture, won by *Gentleman's Agreement*.

Unknown: Ritter's next roles were uncredited – the 1948 noir, at left, and the 1949 comedy drama, below.

The Good, the Not-So- Good and the Uncredited

Kasia Orzazewski: excellent   **Helen Walker**: gone   **E.G. Marshall:** uncredited.

Call Northside 777 is a good movie, but its structure lets it down. The long scene of the lie detector breaks the tension. Helen Walker as P.J.'s wife impresses in Act 1 but disappears for Acts 2 and 3. The voice-over spoke only at the beginning and end. Noir stylistics float in and out. As a positive, Director Henry Hathaway got good performances from the entire cast. Of note was the unknown Kasia Orzazewski, who plays a Polish mother who has scrubbed floors for 11 years, saving every cent to prove her son's innocence. Broadway actor E.G. Marshall was uncredited in his fourth film.

Thelma Ritter is on the record for an uncredited role in *Call Northside 777*. The record says she plays a secretary. One source said she appears in a "blink and you miss it" moment. I must have blinked as I missed it. I agree with another source who said Thelma fell from the film to the cutting-room floor.

No Word of a lie: Richard Conte, good as a 99-year convict, and Leonarde Keeler.

Among the uncredited actors was Leonarde Keeler, the co-inventor of the lie detector. Movie database, IMDb, says Keeler insisted he play the scene as no actor could use the polygraph machine properly. Who knows? Maybe he just wanted to be in a movie. While the scene was interesting with Keeler demonstrating how a lie detector worked, it went on for too long and broke the suspense.

In 1930, Keeler and forensic scientist and pilot Katherine Kay Applegate wed. In the late 1930s, the marriage was in trouble, and Keeler began to drink and smoke heavily. Kay left him in 1940. She died on a solo flight in November 1944.
– Storiesbehindthestars.org

Kay's leaving him and her death exacerbated Keeler's self-medication with alcohol and nicotine. He died of a stroke in 1949, a year after the release of *Call Northside 777*. He was 45 years old.

Kay Applegate's life is quite the story. She was the world's first forensic scientist. She set up a woman-only detective agency. Applegate was an air-force squadron leader in World War II. That no-one has made a biopic about Applegate surprises me.

As barfly Anna Felczak, Jane Crowley turned in a credible performance, but alas, was uncredited. Crowley's business card must have read, *always working, never credited*. She appeared in eight films released in 1948, including the noir classic *The Snake Pit*. Jane went uncredited in all eight. Crowley's scene at 1:20:44 in *Call Northside 777* is a highlight of the film when James Stewart tries to persuade her to give him the address of the eyewitness against Conte.

"I oughta have one to talk on."

"What's in it for me?"

"She hadn't oughta thrown them bricks at me." (One of the best movie lines ever).

I was going to count the uncredited performances Crowley had in her lengthy career, but I did not have an afternoon to spare. Her first role, uncredited of course, was in 1929's romantic drama *The Dance of Life*. I was fibbing before when I said I could not count Jane's uncredited performance as it was easy. She had seventy-four roles in film and on television. She was uncredited in seventy-four. That's right, all of them. That deserves an Oscar. The Oscar for Always Working, Never Credited goes to . . .

Late to movies: E.G. Marshall in the 1966 neo-noir *The Chase.*

The Player

Thelma Ritter turned 46 in 1948, in February, the month *Call Northside 777* debuted. In her second film role, she was uncredited and, I believe, expunged from the film. An uncredited player in his fourth film was E.G. Marshall, 33, when the movie opened.

Marshall has a brief part in *Call Northside 777.* Jimmy Stewart interviews him as he is the second husband of the woman divorced at the insistence of her first spouse, wrongly convicted of murder. Marshall's soft subdued performance as a decent shy man is quietly compelling.

Little is known about Marshall's life before his Broadway success in his late twenties. He gave false academic credentials and refused to say what E.G. stood for. It was likely Everett Grunz, his birth name. Everett was okay for Hollywood, but Grunz would not do. Broadway success came with Thornton Wilder's *The Skin of Our Teeth* (1942-43) and S.N. Behrman and Franz Werfel's comedy *Jacobowsky and the Colonel* (1944-45).

Marshall was well down the cast list in both productions, but he was an early inductee into the famed Actors Studio, founded in 1947.

Marshall returned to the stage before a juicy bit part as the naval prosecutor of a mad Bogart in *The Caine Mutiny* 1954 led to a Hollywood career. Noir around the edges, the mutiny and the subsequent trial of Commander Queeg captured the imagination of cinema goers and is still held in high regard today.

But one thing that today's viewers might find disconcerting is how the story turns around to make the whistleblower, played by Fred MacMurray, the villain while the mad ship's captain becomes a victim of battle fatigue.

After *The Caine Mutiny*, it was strawberries and cream for Marshall. He played in the Oscar-winning Western *Broken Lance* 1954 (Philip Yordan for Best Story). He had a bigger role in the exceptionally good noir *Pushover*, the same year. His other films released in 1954 were the Korean-war drama *The Bamboo Prison*, and a bit of historical nonsense *The Silver Chalice*, with a wasted Oscar-winning score by Franz Waxman.

Marshall followed in a slice of quasi-religious puffery, *The Left Hand of God* 1955. We were not sure whether the title referred to Lucifer or Humphrey Bogart playing a sinner turned saint. As Bogie almost said in *Casablanca*, "If we gave it any thought, we still would not care." *The Scarlet Hour* 1956 was a disappointing noir from producer/ director Michael Curtiz (*Casablanca, Mildred Pierce*).

Trivia

What's up with that? In *The Scarlet Hour*, E. G. Marshall plays a Police Lt. Jennings. Male lead Tom Tryon, pictured above with Carol Ohmart, plays E. V. Marshall. Oh, and Ohmart was Armelia Carol's real family name. It was the Mormon's first film, and the imposed femme fatality was too much for her. Tryon was also making his debut.

Cannot rise above poor script: *The Mountain* climbers include William Demarest, Spencer Tracy, Claire Trevor, being un-Trevor-like, Jim Hayward, and E.G.

The Mountain 1956 never reached great dramatic heights, despite some attractive cinematography from Franz Planer.

Robert Wagner, right, and Tracy are brothers. You must admit there is an uncanny resemblance and a barely discernible difference in ages.

The Mountain cost $2.1 million in pre-blockbuster currency and lost money.

I have never been comfortable at a bucks night, the Australian idiom for the American bachelor party. For starters, where do you put the apostrophe? Is it bucks' night or buck's night, or do you leave it out entirely? Anyway, I have never seen E.G.'s next film, the 1957 drama *Bachelor Party*, the 1984 comedy *Bachelor Party*, the 2018 parody or the 2024 Indian version. Enough with the bachelor parties, already.

The above is my saying I have not watched any of them, nor am I inclined to do so.

E.G. Marshall plays the oldest member of the 1957 BP. He has a bad case of asthma and is one of four middle-class miserable or frightened men at the party. The fifth man is a swinging bachelor, putting on a front to mask loneliness. Sounds depressing. Enough to make you an angry man. There were twelve of them in E.G.'s classic that followed.

Angry guys R us 12: #1 Martin Balsam (foreman, footy coach), #2 John Fiedler – bank clerk, #3 Lee J. Cobb – small business owner, #4 E.G. Marshall – stockbroker, #5 Jack Klugman (paramedic, risen above poverty) #6 Edward Binns – house painter, #7 Jack Warden – salesman, #8 Henry Fonda – architect, #9 Joseph Sweeney – retired, #10 Ed Begley (repair shop owner, bigot) #11 George Voskovec (watchmaker, European emigrant) #12 Robert Webber – advertising executive.

E.G. Marshall's most iconic film role was as an unemotional analytical stockbroker, a cool head among the passionate characters in the 1957 courtroom drama *12 Angry Men*. The movie was a reprise of the 1954 Reginald Rose teleplay and 1955 San Francisco stage play. Although we tend to think of films devolving into television productions, Hollywood rebirthed teleplays as classic feature films. Examples are the romantic dramas *Marty* 1955 and *The Rainmaker* 1956, the noirs *Dragnet* 1954 and *Bad Day at Black Rock* 1955, the comedy *The Reluctant Debutante* 1958 and the neo-noir *Requiem for a Heavyweight* 1962. Two of the angry 12 of the 1954 teleplay returned for the 1957 movie: Joseph Sweeney and George Voskovec. Three other teleplay stars were Robert Cummings – juror #8, Franchot Tone – juror #3, and Edward Arnold – juror # 10. Arnold died in April 1956.

The company that produced the 1955 play, Dramatic Publishing, created the revisionist versions, *12 Angry Jurors* and *12 Angry Women*. Professionals and amateurs recreated the play over the 70 years since the film's tepidly received cinematic debut. Papers by jurists, ethicists, and even sales professionals have examined the film.

The verdict: *12 Angry Men* ★★★★⯪

Mum, pal, and wife: Connie Gilchrist, Thelma Ritter, and Linda Darnell in *A Letter to Three Wives.*

Thelma Ritter was uncredited again in the comedy-drama *A Letter to Three Wives* 1949, but it was her most substantial role so far in films. Joseph L. Mankiewicz was the writer/director. He was so impressed with Ritter's performance that he wrote the role of Birdie Coonan in *All About Eve* 1950 with Ritter in mind, and he lobbied for her inclusion in that film.

In *A Letter to Three Wives*, Ritter plays Sadie Dugan, the wise-cracking down-to -earth assistant to wife Ann Sothern and friend to wife Linda Darnell. Ritter shares juicy scenes with Connie Gilchrist playing Darnell's poor but proud Irish mother. Jeanne Crain was the third wife.

Sis and daughter:

Barbara Lawrence is Darnell's sister and Gilchrist's daughter.

Paul Douglas plays Linda Darnell's older husband, who is unsure if she really loves him. A latecomer to films, after 20 years voicing newsreels, Douglas landed this good role in only his second film. He moved between comedy and noirs like *Panic in the Streets* 1950, *Fourteen Hours* 1951, *Clash by Night* 1952 (an underappreciated movie) and *Joe Macbeth* 1955 (a British Shakespearean noir that surprisingly works okay). Unfortunately, Douglas, 52, died from a heart attack in 1959.

Good lines

Connie Gilchrist: Can't we have peace in this house even on New Year's Eve?
Thelma Ritter: You got it mixed up with Christmas. New Year's Eve is when people go back to killing each other.

Thelma Ritter: You know what I like about your (radio) program? Even when I'm running the vacuum, I can understand it.
Ann Sothern: Thank you so much.

Paul Douglas: To you, I'm a cash register. You can't love a cash register.
Linda Darnell: And I'm part of your inventory. You can't love that, either.

The verdict: *A Letter to Three Wives* 

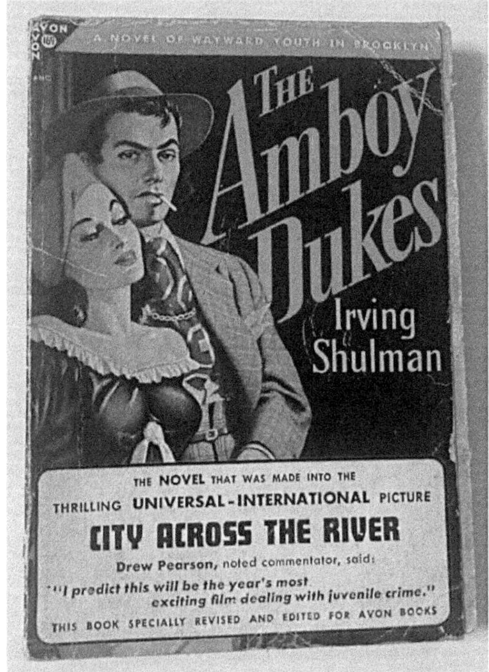

The 1949 noir *City Across the River* is too preachy and undermines its aim of realistically portraying people of an impoverished area of Brooklyn. Thelma Ritter as an Irish mother almost succeeds in rendering pathos from a melodramatic script, but the faux realism wears down the viewer's interest.

That is right – Ritter plays Katie Cusack, the mother of the central character Frank Cusack from a 1947 novel about a Jewish youth gang. In the novel, Ritter's character is Sarah Goldfarb. In the movie poster, you will see the gang as "The Dukes", omitting Amboy, a street in the Jewish neighborhood of Brooklyn. The book sold millions, so its readers, as well as Brooklyn residents, must have been confused by the characters' mass conversion to Catholicism and name changes. Talking of name changes, the cast member Anthony Curtis is Tony Curtis in his first credited role. Bernard Schwartz, TC's birth name, grew up in Manhattan and wisely does not affect a Brooklyn accent. He is appealing as the most sensitive member of the gang.

The change to Irish characters did not wreck the movie, but it was a contribution to inauthenticity. The condescending rave about juvenile delinquency from journalist Drew Pearson did not inspire expectations of an objective presentation. The juvenile delinquency "problem" in the U.S during World War II ended after the war, but not for populist politicians and sensationalist or moralistic filmmakers.
Ritter crossed the river for her next film, a satirical classic. 

Chapter 7: It's all about Margo

Producers Sol Siegel and Darryl F. Zanuck were optimistic for *A Letter to Three Wives*, and the film justified expectations with a Best Picture nomination and wins by Joseph L. Mankiewicz for directing and adapted screenplay. Mankiewicz realized that Thelma Ritter's supporting role as Ann Sothern's mouthy help contributed to the movie's success. He wrote a part for Ritter as Bette Davis's loyal but mouthy assistant in:

Except it is not *All About Eve*. Not at all. It is all about Margo Channing, the aging Broadway star who hides her insecurities behind acidic wit inspired by a love of words and a penchant for spite. Ritter is Margo's assistant, Birdie Coonan. The pair trade barbs, but you can feel the bonds of affection between them. With *All About Eve*, Mankiewicz wrote one of the wittiest of Hollywood screenplays. And one of the cleverest, as he pitches jests at varying intellectual levels, so no viewer feels alienated from the humor. Who can resist a laugh when Margo looks directly at egotistical theater critic Addison DeWitt (George Sanders) and bites off a piece of celery?

When we first meet Margo Channing's devoted fan Eve Harrington (Anne Baxter), we find the younger woman a bit weird in going to every one of the actor's performances and hanging around the stage door to grab a glimpse of her idol. But we and everyone in Margo's entourage believe her intentions are good. Except for Birdie Coonan.

"How do you do, my dear," Margo says to Eve.

"Oh, brother," Birdie interjects. "When she gets like this, all of a sudden she's playing Hamlet's mother."

Anyone familiar with the play thinks Birdie's rudeness is down to jealousy, a theme in *Hamlet*. But *Hamlet* is also about regicide. Ritter, like a *Macbeth* witch, predicts the plot.

"Eddie wasn't coming at all. Eddie was dead."

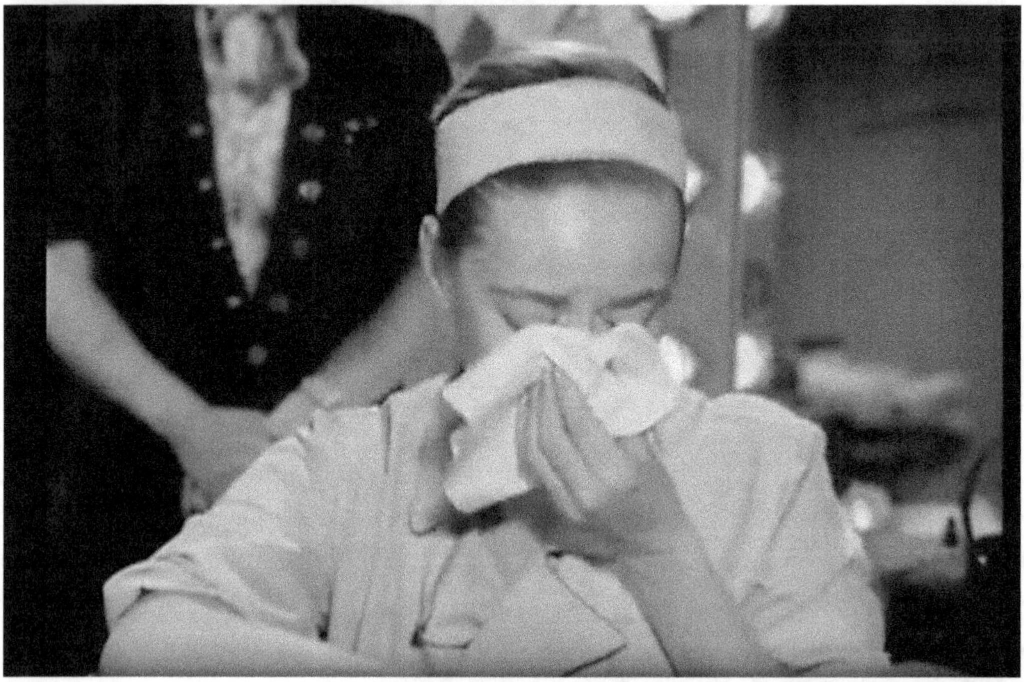

"What a story! Everything but the bloodhounds snapping at her rear end."

The 1951 Academy Awards brought surprises. That Mankiewicz won best director and best adapted screenplay were not among them. He had received the double for *A Letter to Three Wives*, and *All About Eve* was a significantly superior film. The surprises were that Davis and Baxter received nominations for best female actor, and Ritter and Celeste Holm had nominations for best female support.

Holm is very good as Margo's galpal Karen who is a generous champion of nerdy Eve. But what an unenviable task for Academy voters to choose between her and Ritter for the Oscar. It went to Josephine Hull for an admirable performance in the comedy drama *Harvey* 1950.

It was a similar story for the best lead that neither Davis nor Baxter won. Judy Holliday took it for *Born Yesterday: My Fair Lady,* with the addition of a wealthy junkyard owner. *Born Yesterday* was an affable comedy, but it did not require the standard of acting set by other nominees, Davis, Baxter, and Gloria Swanson in *Sunset Boulevard*. *All About Eve* won best picture while Mankiewicz took the director's award from the best field of films to ever vie for the directorial Oscar.

Left, George Cukor

Below John Huston

Billy Wilder

Carol Reed

The eyes have it:

Bette Davis was 5ft 2in (158cm) tall and of small stature, certainly not the classic beauty that stars are made of or are made over to become.

But the toughness in her movie persona and her voice combined to great effect. Those qualities and her acting talents made her a perennial A-lister for decades.

Then there were those eyes, most remarkable, they should write a song about them. Hey wait, they did, in 1974, Donna Terry Weiss and Jackie DeShannon did it. Kim Carne rendered a suitably tough version in 1981, and *Bette Davis Eyes* was a worldwide hit.

In 1961, director Frank Capra explained why he was remaking his 1933 sentimental comedy drama *Lady for a Day*, thirty years later. The original had received a stack of Academy Award nominations but was winless. It returned multiples of its $300,000 budget, and Capra was on 10 per cent of the net profit. Why wasn't he at home reflecting on past glory and counting his money? "I wanted to remake the picture with harder people. Well, she's about as hard as you can get." – Stine W. and Davis B. *Mother Goddam: The Story of the Career of Bette Davis With a Running Commentary by Bette Davis* (great title) Prentice-Hall, Ontario, 1974, page 3.

Of course, Capra meant Bette Davis in his remake *A Pocketful of Miracles* 1961.

Davis concurred, "Hollywood hates me, and I hate Hollywood. I'm not going back there to play a sentimental old hag . . . a bitchy part, yes."

Capra F. *The Name Above the Title*, MacMillan, N.Y., 1971, page 475.

A Pocketful of Miracles, which Capra made during bouts of excruciating headaches, lost money. Not because the advent of the Swinging Sixties had passed by Capra, 64, and Davis, 53. But because Capra had compromised on his vision, to take what seemed like the easier buck. "Don't compromise. For only the valiant can create. Only the Daring should make films. – Capra F. page 486. The next year, Davis was Oscar-nominated for *Whatever Happened to Baby Jane?*, a comic horror film about former stars.

In *Whatever Happened to Baby Jane?*, Davis plays the former child star in the title. Jane never made the transition from vaudeville to films, but her older sister Blanche (Joan Crawford) became a Hollywood star before a hit-and-run driver crippled her. The casting played on the rivalry of the two noir stars, a rivalry they denied, contrary to evidence such as Crawford campaigning against Davis's Baby Jane Oscar nomination and arranging to receive the Oscar on behalf of the eventual winner, Anne Bancroft, for *The Miracle Worker* 1960.

Unlike Baby Jane, Davis was not a child star. After her parents' divorce in 1915, her mother, earning meagre wages, sent Bette to a modest boarding school. As a teenager in New York, Davis became a Girl Scout, rising to the position of patrol leader. Not the stuff of stardom unless you count evening campfires. Davis was not a prodigy, and she was 21 years old before her first stage role. Within a year, she had appeared on Broadway and had moved to Hollywood.

Davis had an inauspicious start in *Bad Sister* 1931. The lead was cinematic heartthrob Conrad Nagel, and the cinematographer was expressionist Karl Freund (*The Golem* 1920, *The Last Laugh* 1924, *Metropolis* 1927). Despite these talents, the movie, summed up in two words, was: "bad, sister".

Davis followed with a forgettable minor role in *Seed* 1931, and Universal was about to cut her loose when thin praise from Freund saved her: "She has nice eyes."
– Stine W. and Davis B. page 12. Those Bette Davis eyes.

Eighteen movies quickly followed before her breakout role in *Of Human Bondage* 1934, based on a novel by Somerset Maugham. She was the female lead to Leslie Howard, and John Cromwell directed. Her best film before Bondage was a proto-noir *Three on a Match* 1932 which critics panned on its release but acclaimed on reevaluations.

In *Of Human Bondage*, Davis gives a searing performance as a working-class waiter who rejects the love of a middle-class medical student.

Proto-noir *Bordertown* 1935 was a success for Warners. Funnily enough, Ida Lupino's role in Warners' 1940 noir *They Drive by Night* was eerily similar to Davis's in the earlier film. As the wit Dorothy Parker quipped, "The only ism Hollywood believes in is plagiarism." Also in 1935, Davis won the Academy Award she should have received for *Of Human Bondage*. The "best actress" Oscar was for *Dangerous*, a film I could never warm to after Franchot Tone tells Davis her performance as Juliet inspired him to become an architect. What, he wanted to design balconies? Juliet is the sunshade.

Another proto-noir followed. *The Petrified Forest* 1936 reunited Davis with Leslie Howard and *Bordertown* director Archie Mayo. Humphrey Bogart's role as escaped criminal Duke Mantee should have alerted Warners to Bogie's star power. But Warners had only hired him at Howard's insistence, and the studio was convinced Bogart was strictly B-material. It took six years for Jack Warner to wise up after the success of *High Sierra* 1941 and *The Maltese Falcon* 1941. *Bordertown* lead Paul Muni and George Raft had rejected the *High Sierra* and *The Maltese Falcon* roles Bogie seized.

In the boxing proto-noir *Kid Galahad* 1937, Davis, as a victim of unrequited love, took the acting honors ahead of Edward G. Robinson and Humphrey Bogart.

As with *Dangerous*, Davis played another baddie turned goodie in *Jezebel* 1938. The Academy said, "That's fair enough, have another Academy Award." The studios got the best of both worlds. Davis wins the Oscar for being a horrible devious person, but they do not need to offend her fans by killing her off in the last reel, as the studios had to do in the 1940s and 50s with their noir femme fatales. Luckily for Barbara Stanwyck and Claire Trevor, reincarnation followed 1944's *Double Indemnity* and *Murder, My Sweet*.

Davis started the 1940s in fine style with the top noir *The Letter* 1940, the even better drama *The Little Foxes* 1941 and the comedy *The Man Who Came to Dinner* 1942. From there, it was downhill, though the drama *Now Voyager* 1942 had its moments, and the soggy wartime melodrama *Watch on the Rhine* 1943 won awards.

Davis's last noir of the 1940s was the disappointing *Deception* 1946. It looked as if her career was in decline until along came the noir satire *All About Margo*, I apologize, *All About Eve*. I would like to say she kicked on in the 1950s, but it would not be true. Davis had a smaller role in the 1953 noir *Phone Call from a Stranger*, contrived and unpleasant. *Storm Center* 1956 was a worthy, but dull in parts, polemic against book banning. In today's social climate, it is a viable choice for retro film festivals.

Never mind the 1950s decline, there will always be Margo and her mouthy bud, Birdie.

"Fasten your seat belts," Margo Channing warned. "It's going to be a bumpy night."

That is just one of the memorable lines from one of the wittiest movies ever made.

Great lines

Margo has more from where that came:

Forty. Four oh - That slipped out. I hadn't quite made up my mind to admit it. Now I suddenly feel as if I've taken all my clothes off. (Bette was forty-two when Eve opened).

So many people know me. I wish I did. I wish someone would tell me about me.

(To Eve) **You can always** put that award where your heart ought to be.

Birdie tweets harshly:

She's studying you like you was a play or a book or a set of blueprints, how you walk, talk, eat, think, sleep. (Among all the theatrical celebrities, "slave labor" Birdie is the wise one).

Next to a tenor, a wardrobe woman is the touchiest thing in show business.

There's some loose characters dressed like maids and butlers. Who'd you call - the William Morris (talent) Agency?

As for bein' fifth-rate - I closed the first half for eleven years an' you know it! (Birdie is telling us she was a vaudeville performer given the prestigious job as the last act before intermission. We imagine Birdie as an acerbic comedian).

Karen Richards (Celeste Holm) chimes in.

It's about time Margo realized that what's attractive on stage need not necessarily be attractive off.

Addison DeWitt drips vitriol.

Margo is a great Star. A true star. She never was or will be anything less or anything else. (DeWitt is a second-rate Oscar Wilde who bathes in acid).

But Miss Caswell (Marilyn Monroe) has DeWitt's measure. (DeWitt says he has only met Eve in passing) Miss Caswell: **That's how** you met me... in passing.

(Eve says she will bore DeWitt) Miss Caswell: **You won't** bore him, honey. You won't even get a chance to talk.

Bill Sampson (Gary Merrill): **Wherever there's magic** and make-believe and an audience, there's theater. Donald Duck, Ibsen and the Lone Ranger. Sarah Bernhardt and Poodles Hanneford, Lunt and Fontanne, Betty Grable, Rex the Wild Horse, Eleonora Duse, all theater. You don't understand them all. You don't like them all. Why should you?
(Poodles was a bareback riding clown).

Mank Mk II: Joseph L. Mankiewicz with Marilyn Monroe, left, and older brother, Herman J., below.

All About Eve screenwriter/ director Joseph L. Mankiewicz was a cinematic polymath. He started as a screenwriter with Paramount, moved into production at MGM, had a fight with Louis B. Mayer, who would not allow him to direct, and he went to Fox for the opportunity. That was in 1944, and he kept writing all through the progression.

Joseph was the younger brother of Herman, co-writer, with Orson Welles, of *Citizen Kane* 1941, the innovative noirish film, directed by and starring Welles.

The 2020 biopic *Mank* is entertaining, though I am not convinced of its historical accuracy about the closeness of Herman to newspaper baron, William Randolph Hearst's mistress, actor Marion Davies.

Despite alcoholism, Mank was a prolific contributor to films, often comedies or satires. He was 55 years old when he died.

Joseph L. Mankiewicz was co-writer, with Oliver H. P. Garrett and Donald Ogden Stewart, of the 1934 crime movie, *Manhattan Melodrama*. It was the first of fourteen movies, such as the Thin Man films, with Myrna Loy and William Powell, and one of Mickey Rooney's first films. It was the film that gangster John Dillinger watched before Federal agents gunned him to death outside Chicago's Biograph Theater.

Mankiewicz produced Fritz Lang's first American film, the proto-noir *Fury* 1936 and a series of Joan Crawford romantic comedies including *The Bride Wore Red* 1937, directed by Dorothy Arzner.

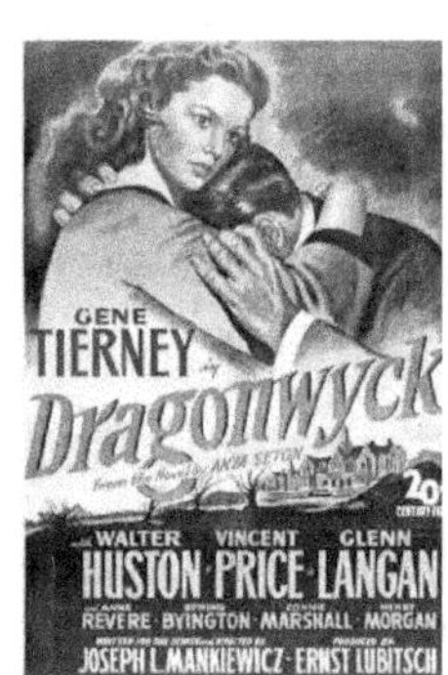

Mankiewicz produced a string of successes for MGM, including the romantic comedies *The Philadelphia Story 1940* and *Woman of the Year 1942*, before his first directorial effort for Fox, the period drama *Dragonwyck* 1946, also a box-office winner. *Somewhere in the Night* 1946, an amnesiac noir he co-wrote with Howard Dimsdale and Lee Strasberg, was director Mankiewicz's first venture in the genre. It was okay. The posters were good. Nancy Guild was not a good actor.

The noirs *House of Strangers* 1949 and *No Way Out* 1950 that preceded *All About Eve* were of much better quality than his first noir. *House of Strangers* shone as a Godfather precursor with Richard Conte delivering a career-best performance. Conte was rewarded 23 years later with a plum support in *The Godfather*.

Suspect grammar: Are not lust, passion, greed, and desire redundant? A grammarian did not design this poster, which is attractive, but a little crowded. I presume the title refers to 5-finger discount, aka theft.

Mankiewicz received an Oscar nomination for the 1952 spy noir, *5 Fingers*. Co-star Danielle Darrierux was a famed French actor who worked for eighty years from 1930. She died from a fall in 2017, five months after turning one hundred. She rarely ventured from Europe for filming, but Mank the Younger persuaded her to come to America. Producers decided to shoot the film, based on a true story of a Turkish spy, in Hollywood. Mankiewicz did take a small crew to Ankara for location shots, which is more than Hollywood did for *Algiers* 1938 and *Casablanca* 1942.

Mankiewicz achieved what eludes most film makers: his last two films were top notch. He shared directing with Sydney Lumet for the doco *King* 1970, and he received an Oscar nomination for directing *Sleuth* 1972, the film adaptation of Anthony Shaffer's clever thriller of a play, with Shaffer writing the film script.

Chapter 8: Second nom is comic

Thelma Ritter zoomed up to fourth lead in the comedy, *The Mating Season* 1951. When the show business concluded, Thel gave enough for another best support nomination. As with other movies from 1930 to 1950, *The Mating Season* transformed from a play. It made sense for talkies to use plays, a medium that lives or dies on the spoken word. Hollywood also enticed the speakers of those words from New York, San Francisco, and Chicago for a fraction of the price silent stars had earned.

New York Times, December 11, 1950, Page 31.

What was unusual was that Caesar Dunn's play *Maggie*, cloned into *The Mating Season*, had not made Broadway. Paramount parted with twenty-five large for a play that had a try-out in Florida in 1949.

Dunn's first Broadway play was the farce *What the Doctor Ordered* 1927, produced and directed by future noir director John Cromwell (*Algiers* 1938, *Dead Reckoning* 1947, *Caged* 1950). Studios blacklisted Cromwell shortly after *Caged*. His film before the backlisting was another noir *The Racket* 1951, about gangsters, but it could have been about populist politicians engaging in witch-hunts.

The Mating Season is from the lineage of the play of misunderstanding, a cuz of the farce, a genre I dislike, especially the British or British inspired variety. I find them of infinite sameness. Only parts of the plots change to protect the guilty playwrights.

The Mating Season mixes misunderstanding with "fish out of water" comedy and romance. The best said about leads Gene Tierney and John Lund is that their characters are affable newlyweds. Ritter as the groom's fishy mother, and 1930s dramatic star Miriam Hopkins as the snobbish mother of the bride, do the light lifting of comedy. Hopkins and Ritter save the film, though their dialog was not sharp enough to my taste.

Ritter pretends to be a domestic to be near her son. The best scene is when Hopkins raids the fridge late at night and overhears what she construes as a romantic assignation between Lund and Ritter.

The weakest part of the movie was the rendering of the compulsory "boy loses girl" contrivance, weak tea, indeed. The year before, writer/ producer Charles Brackett was responsible for the scintillating dialog of *Sunset Boulevard*, so this was quite a let-down from that film.

The Player

Miriam Hopkins was a chorus girl and theatrical actor in New York before she got her start in movies during the liberal pre-code era.

The Hays Code was introduced in 1930 but was not enforced until 1934 after the arrival of Catholic layman Joseph I Breen, below, as chief censor.

Three Hopkins' movies Joe Breen would have butchered:

Dr. Jekyll and Mr. Hyde 1931.

Trouble in Paradise 1932.

The Story of Temple Drake 1933.

Fred and Mirriam: Fredrich March and Hopkins in *Dr. Jekyll and Mr. Hyde*.

What evil lurks in the hearts and minds of the censorial and the greedy? Censors forced Paramount to cut eight minutes from Jekyll and Hyde. New York producers filmed the story in 1912 and 1913. The first Hollywood adaptation of Robert Louis Stevenson's novel appeared in 1920 and starred John Barrymore. MGM released a sanitized remake, starring Spencer Tracy, in 1941. The greedy studio tried to round up and destroy all the prints of the 1920 and 1931 versions. As with *Nosferatu: A Symphony of Horror* 1922 and *The Long Night* 1947, the censors and the greedy studios failed. The 1931 version of *Dr. Jekyll and Mr. Hyde* is available on DVD and Blu-ray. Critics regard the 1931 effort as better than the one released ten years later. You can decide for yourself.

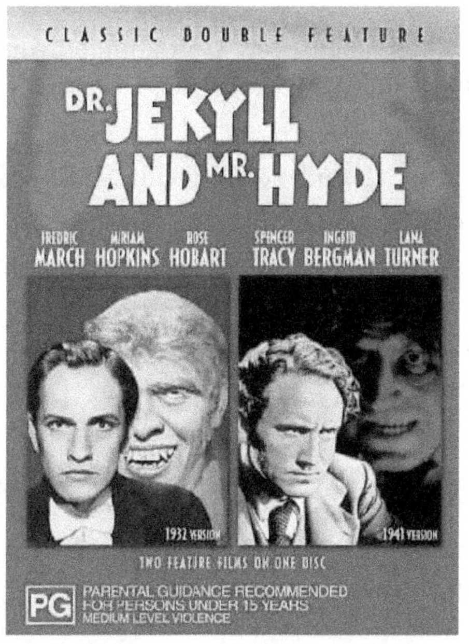

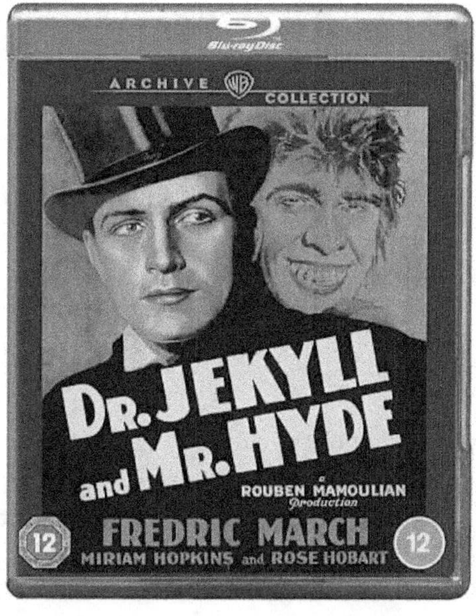

Double Trouble: Herbert Marshall with Kay Francis and Hopkins

In 1935, Paramount applied for the reissue of *Trouble in Paradise* 1932. Joe Breen cried, permission denied. Paramount proposed a musical version in 1943. Joe Breen cried, permission denied. The movie reappeared on screens in 1968. In a 1998 review, esteemed critic Roger Ebert wrote, "The sexual undertones are surprisingly frank in this pre-Code 1932 film, and we understand that none of the three characters is in any danger of mistaking sex for love." You see why Catholic layman Breen hated it: three people were having fun. Worse, they were not feeling at all guilty about it.

Naughty things they said:

Gaston Monescu (Marshall): So, you think you can get me?
Madame Colet (Francis)*:* Any minute I want.
Monescu: You're conceited.
Madame Colet: But attractive.

Monescu: Madame Colet, if I were your father, which fortunately I am not, and you made any attempt to handle your own business affairs, I would give you a good spanking - in a business way, of course.

Lily (Hopkins): I love you as a crook. I worship you as a crook. Steal, swindle, rob. Oh, but don't become one of those useless, good-for-nothing gigolos.

Madame Colet: Don't be so down-hearted, Major. You're not the only one I don't love. I don't love Francois either.

Lily: I have a confession to make to you. Baron, you are a crook. You robbed the gentleman.
Monescu: The wallet of the gentleman is in your possession. I knew it very well when you took it out of my pocket. In fact, you tickled me. But your embrace was so sweet.

Trivia: As a teenager, Kay Francis attended Miss Fuller's School for Young Ladies in a small village in New York State. Sounds a perfect alma mater for a romcom star.

The Story of Temple Drake 1933 is a pivotal film in the conversion of the lame-duck Hays Office to a 40-year censorship authority under Joseph I. Breen. Will Hays, whose name became attached to the Motion Picture Production Code, said he would prohibit any film version of William Faulkner's novel *Sanctuary* 1930. Surprisingly, Joe Breen, then working in publicity for the Hays Office, in a memo dated 7 Mar 1933, defended the film. He said it was mild compared to the novel. Showing the talent that would make him chief censor, Breen added he had never read the book.

– *AFI CATALOG OF FEATURE FILMS THE FIRST 100 YEARS 1893–1993.*

The producers adjusted the script to soften the rape scene at the centre of the novel and film. Joe Breen said the picture watered down the novel, the title of which is not in the opening credits. What should receive credit is how the film gives nuance to Hopkins' portrayal of southern debutante Temple Drake, whom Faulkner portrayed as a misogynist trope of a young woman inviting rape by the way she dresses and acts.

Hopkins regarded *The Story of Temple Drake* as the best film she ever made. She seized on the complexity of the character she described as an "unstandardized wretch". "Give me the complicated ladies and I'll interpret the daylights out of them."
Ellenberger A.R. *Miriam Hopkins: Life and Films of a Hollywood Rebel* 2018, University Press of Kentucky, page 85.

With his promotion to chief censor in 1934, Joe Breen back-pedalled on his assessment of the film after its successful 1934 run. He was appeasing his boss, Will Hays. Miriam Hopkins was wise to Breen: "There was talk of reissuing it, but it couldn't get by the censors." – Ellenberger A.R. page 85.

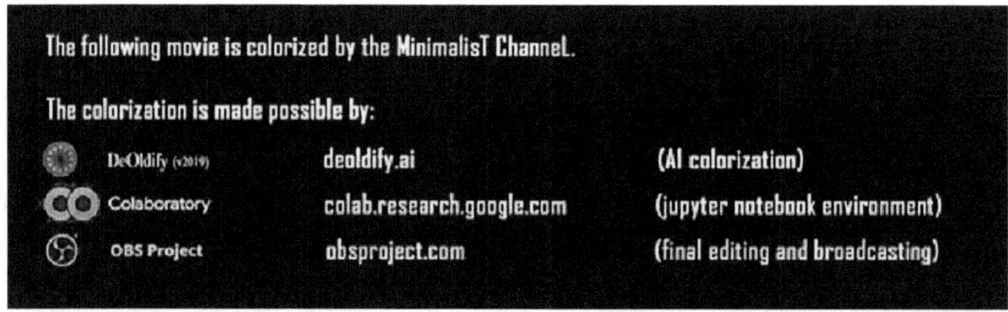

The Story of Temple Drake reappeared in 2011, when a restoration by the Museum of Modern Art screened at the TCM Classic Film Festival. The Criterion Channel sells Blu-ray and DVDs with added features.

Vandals broke in and colorized one version.

Trivia

Jack La Rue had his first leading role as Temple's rapist. But it did not advance his career, though he was a bit player in many movies. In England, he again landed the lead in *No Orchids for Miss Blandish*, based on the 1939 novel by popular crime writer James Hadley Chase. The author made no secret of the fact that he lifted large chunks from Faulkner's *Sanctuary*. Did La Rue have more success from an association with *Sanctuary*, the second time around? No Orchids did well at the box office. The punters lined up to watch what critics universally called the worst British film ever made because of its brutality, perversion, sex, and sadism. The only demand censors made of the filmmakers was to cut back a kiss from 45 seconds to 20 seconds. Censors are funny.

Chapter 9: Late bloomers feel young

The leads of this 1951 film, Monty Wooley and Thelma had in common arriving late to film and receiving unsuccessful Oscar noms.

Wooley, born in 1888, was an English and drama teacher before he directed his first Broadway play in 1929. A decade later he tasted success on Broadway starring in *The Man Who came to Dinner*. He emulated that role and that success in the 1941 film version.

Wooley's Oscar nominations were for wartime dramas, best actor for *The Pied Pier* 1943 and best support for *Since You Went Away* 1945.

Balancing the older leads are two young offscreen galpals in support roles – Jean Peters and Marilyn Monroe. Peters and Monroe would be together again with substantial roles in the flawed color noir *Niagara* 1953. That same year, Peters and Thelma Ritter would give excellent performances in the noir classic *Pickup on South Street*, directed by Samuel Fuller and starring Richard Widmark.

The second male lead in *As Young as You Feel* was David Wayne. In a surprise pick, Wayne was cast as the child murderer in Joseph Losey's 1951 remake of Fritz Lang's *M* 1931 with Peter Lorre in the lead. Audiences would have been surprised to see David Wayne in those disparate roles in 1951.

As Young as You Feel is an amiable if slight comedy about a business losing respect for senior workers. The film won me over early with Thelma Ritter's spirited defense of Brooklyn, made even more endearing as it was apropos of nothing. "The first thing you know, somebody will remind me that I came from Brooklyn. But first, I would like to remind them that some of the finest people in the world came from Brooklyn."

2+2=4: If Jean Peters marries David Wayne, they will have four first names between them.

Peters shows herself to be a dab hand at comedy in a role unlike others she had played.

As you might expect, Monty Wooley was adept at vocal and physical humor, a capacity he shared with Ritter. While not the most memorable of comedies, it makes you as young as you feel good.

The verdict: ★★★⯪☆

Chapter 10: There was a third nom: she did not get it

Thelma Ritter's third Academy Award nomination was for *With a Song in My Heart* 1952, the sentimental biopic about singer Jane Froman, a huge radio and concert star from the 1930s. One of her signature tunes gave the film its title.

On her way to perform for U.S. troops in 1943, Froman's plane crashed, killing more than half the passengers and severely injuring Froman (Susan Hayward) and her future husband. Ritter plays the nurse who tended to Froman and became her private nurse during the long recovery, which involved more than twenty major operations before the singer could walk with the aid of crutches.

Ritter, pictured above, watches from the wings as Froman performs on a platform attached to a brace attached to a moving piano. Ritter's is a dramatic role, with a few wisecracks and references to Brooklyn. A stirring speech raising the spirits of Froman, downhearted after twenty surgeries, would have bolstered Ritter's prospects for that nomination.

Jane Froman sang the songs for the movie and the subsequent hit record, and she was a technical advisor for the film. Therein lies the problem, at least for this viewer. Everyone is too "nice". David Wayne, who gives a convincing performance as a jealous first husband, morphs into a good guy in the third act.

Susan Hayward does an excellent job in performing the songs dubbed by Ms. Froman. The productions around the songs are elaborate. But are we watching a concert movie or a drama about reaction to a serious accident that threatens the removal of a limb?

The two strands sort of blend together, as does the unusual triple voice-over of Wayne, Ritter, and second hubby Rory Calhoun. The noble changeover over of husbands is unconvincing. The second marriage failed but the divorce was years after the movie.

Susan Hayward and Rory Calhoun, though never together, were in excellent noirs, *Deadline at Dawn* 1946, *The Red House* 1946, *House of Strangers* 1949, and the Oscar-winning *I Want to Live* 1958.

Investigators: Hayward and Paul Lukas.

Hayward's first noir *Deadline at Dawn* has good name-dropping for you to bore fellow guests at a dinner party. It is based on a 1944 novel by **William Irish**, a pseudonym for prolific noir writer **Cornell Woolrich**. Social-realist playwright **Clifford Odets** was the screenwriter. Group Theatre co-founder **Harold Clurman** was the director of this, his only film. The composer of the East German national anthem, a short-lived number, **Hanns Eisler** scored.

It always amazes critics overlook *The Red House* in best-noir votes. This Freudian-drenched horror noir has excellent acting by established stars Edward G, Robinson and Judith Anderson, the former Mrs. Danvers from *Rebecca* 1940. Rory Calhoun, in his second credited role, and Julie London, in her third credited part, ably assist the stars.

The script by Delmer Daves and Albert Maltz, who later was one of the blacklisted Hollywood Ten imprisoned, is clever, telling parallel stories leading up to the revelation of the secret haunting the red house. ★★★★⯪

Bad for each other: Bad boy Rory Calhoun with the wannabe daring Julie London.

The superb noir *House of Strangers* has mentions in film-noir dispatches even fewer times than *The Red House*. The 1949 film includes a career-best performance from noir regular Richard Conte, pictured with Susan Hayward, who tries to save him from his worst instincts.

It is a Godfatherly tale of a corrupt banker with three disgruntled sons and an honest fourth son, played by Conte. Director Joseph L. Mankiewicz wrote an intelligent script, wrongly attributed to Philip Yordan. You can read about the how and the why of the misattribution in my book *Film Noir Fate Vs. The Working Stiff*. If you have not seen *House of Strangers*, reward yourself with a viewing.

The harrowing noir *I Want to Live* earned Susan Hayward an Oscar. The film of a woman on death row begins with this preface by existentialist author Albert Camus:

Hayward deserved her Oscar win. Director Robert Wise (noirs *Born to Kill* 1947, *The Set-up* 1949, *The House on Telegraph Hill* 1951, *Odds Against Tomorrow* 1959, and the sci-fi *The Day the Earth Stood Still* 1951) sustained interest in a movie dominated by its star. Academy Award-winning cinematographer Lionel Lindon (*Around the World in 80 Days* 1956) came to the film with noir credentials (*The Blue Dahlia* 1946, *Alias Nick Beal* 1949 and *Quicksand* 1950).

Wise and Lindon were Oscar-nominated as was Don Mankiewicz (son of Herman, nephew of Joseph) and Nelson Gidding for best adapted screenplay. Other nominees were editor William Hornbeck and Gordon E. Sawyer for sound. Without an Oscar, director Wise won a Golden Globe. Hayward emulated her Oscar with a Golden Globe.

The 1953 Oscars

The year 1952 was not the strongest for Hollywood films, as evidenced by the 25th annual Academy Awards of March 19, 1953, at the RKO Pantages.

Pantages opened as a vaudeville theatre at 6233 Hollywood Blvd, in 1930. RKO bought the theatre at a fire sale after two rape trials that critics believe were set up to ruin the previous owner, impresario Alexander Pantages.
– Adler T. *Hollywood and the Mob: Movies, Mafia, Sex and Death*, Bloomsbury, 2011.

Against Thelma Ritter for best female support were Jean Hagen for *Singin' in the Rain*, Colette Marchand for *Moulin Rouge* and Terry Moore for *Come Back, Little Sheba*.

The winner was noir icon Gloria Grahame for an OTT nine minutes in the bloated melodrama *The Bad and the Beautiful*. George Marshall won best adapted screenplay for the B and the B, that had to be for a different version than the one I watched.

Grahame acceptance speech was, "Thank you very much", an improvement on much of the film's dialog.

Chapter 11: Unsinkable Thel

Titanic survivor: Margaret "Maggie" Brown was never called Molly, except by author Gene Fowler after her death. *The Unsinkable Molly Brown* was a musical and film. Thelma Ritter played Maude Young, based on Brown, in 1953's *Titanic*. No record exists of Ritter being called Thel, except by author Bernie Dowling.

I dislike inaccuracies in docufiction of events, but T*itanic* 1953 is an obvious melodrama built on the skeletal framework of the sinking of the luxury liner in 1912. Watching the movie over the years, I never saw it as a realistic dramatization of the tragedy.

Like Thelma Ritter, Titanic lead Clifton Webb was a late bloomer in film. Born in 1889, the stage actor had a handful of film roles in the 1920s. He returned to movies with an acclaimed role in the 1945 noir classic *Laura*. Webb climbed to the top of Hollywood mountain by playing snobs or eccentrics in drama films such as *The Razor's Edge* 1946, the Mr. Belvedere comedies, starting with *Sitting Pretty* 1948, and the blended family comedy *Cheaper by the Dozen* 1950. Myrna Loy played Webb's wife in *Cheaper by the Dozen,* in which they relived the domestic situation of two real-life efficiency experts. Critics did not bother to ask whether the domestic comedy was an authentic portrayal of the historical family.

Mr. Belvedere and Ms. Ivers:

The female lead in *Titanic* was the versatile Barbara Stanwyck, star of film noir, dramas, and comedies.

Pictured left are Stanwyck, as the female lead of *The Strange Love of Martha Ivers* 1946, and Clifton Webb, as Mr. Belvedere from *Sitting Pretty* 1948.

In *Titanic*, Ritter plays the wealthy owner of a lead mine who admits she does not have the demeanor of a rich woman. On deck on a cold evening, she must open her overcoat to display her expensive necklace to show she is monied. The scene is an attractive introduction to a character who is obviously forthright in manner and speech.

Clifton Webb is also rich. He flaunts his wealth by paying a lot to a stranger for his third-class ticket. This fictional Webb was not too bright, as the ship was only two-thirds full on its maiden voyage. The screenwriters overlooked this fact to cater for the dramatic urgency of Webb boarding the ship.

Meanwhile, Stanwyck, playing Webb's wife, is snugly aboard with their two children. Hello, hello, what's going on here, then? Among the voyagers are Richard Basehart as an alcoholic priest and Robert Wagner as a young man bitten by the love bug. Did I mention this was a melodrama?

The marital conflict in *Titanic* dramatically represents a political and philosophical debate that has raged for 150 years, with Barbara Stanwyck an isolationist and Clifton Webb an internationalist. Stanwyck is taking the children back to America, where they will remain forevermore. Stanwyck claims that international marriages never work. She believes the family's jet-setting lifestyle has turned their daughter into "an arrogant little prig". Never mind that Stanwyck ignores or does not know that prig is a British insult, and most Americans would not recognize it, let alone use it.

Unsophisticated Americans would have misheard Stanwyck as using slang for male genitalia, an invective that dates to the 16th century. Naughty Barbara, but not really.

It should not have surprised to see Fox continue the lucrative typecasting of Webb as an elitist, but it was extravagant of the studio to craft the main plot around it.

Viewer sympathy is with Stanwyck even when she destroys Webb with this line, "He's not your son." This is the best moment of the film, preceded by Webb's observation that he knows his wife has a trump card she is waiting to play.

The bridge card game references and visuals date the movie to later than the 1912 Titanic sinking. I could see no relevance to the film other than bridge being a popular game in the U.S. in the 1940s and 1950s before declining sharply as a form of social interaction in the 1960s. The long bridge game gave Thelma Ritter the chance to share her wisdom that you never send the baby to buy the beer. We can all drink to that.

Thelma Ritter is underutilized in *Titanic*. Above, she is buying a ticket in the sweepstakes on when the boat will land at Pier 59 in New York City. It is a blackly humorous moment as we know it will not be landing at all in New York. Ritter's role is as a comic foil, disappointing as we expected more character development after her playful introduction.

What am I doing here?

Richard Basehart, below, and Frances Bergen, right.

The disappointment for Richard Basehart (*He Walked by Night* 1948) was more acute as his role of the suspended alcoholic priest seemed pointless. Similarly, Frances Bergen (wife of ventriloquist Edgar and mum of actor Candice) as a socialite, seemed to be making up the numbers. The Verdict: *Titanic*. ★ ★ ★

B-girl, 1950s breaking? Not break-girl, bar-girl. **Pole dancing?** Oh, forget it.

Pickup on South Street 1953 is the movie for which Thelma Ritter deserved an Oscar. This is the one that should not have got away. Ritter is the aged street hawker selling ties, and information to the police to save up enough money to avoid burial in a pauper's grave. It might have been different if the NY cemetery for the indigent, Potter's Field, was in Brooklyn, but it was on Hart Island in the Bronx. It is an inspired role, and an inspiration for character actors continuing to shine in movies as they grow older.

Jean Peters as the femme fatale prostitute and Richard Widmark as a pickpocket also deliver excellent performances, but Ritter overshadows them. This is the first noir directed by former screenwriter Samuel Fuller. I regard it as the best movie from Fuller, whom French critics later lionized.

The current of cultural leftism has always been strong in France, and the French distributors changed the dubbed dialog of *Pickup on South Street* to turn the Communist spies into drug dealers.

Brianton K. *The failure of anti-communist films and Pickup on South Street* in *Cinemahistoryonline* 30 August 2019.

Fuller lampoons anti-communism, though good bad-guy Widmark is finally convinced to fight back out of respect for Ritter and love for Peters.

Australian academic Kevin Brianton said FBI director J.Edgar Hoover had lunch with Fuller and Fox boss Darryl F. Zanuck to complain about *Pickup on South Street*. Hoover particularly disapproved of Skip's line to the authorities, "You waving the flag at me."
– Brianton K. 2019.

Widmark's tone verged on the contemptuous as he delivered the flag line. This was at a time that Senator Joseph McCarthy and the House Un-American Activities Committee were at the height of their punitive powers, exercised against creatives whom they called subversives or fellow-travellers of subversives.

Zanuck, who had been a scriptwriter in his younger days, defended Fuller. Zanuck said Hoover knew nothing about filmmaking. Fuller had previously been criticized as soft on communism with his 1951 movie *The Steel Helmet*, about the Korean War. Fuller was a World War II close-combat veteran who attained multiple honors. Journalist Victor Riesel called Fuller "pro-Communist" and "anti-American". Riesel had not served during World War II, despite being a year younger than Fuller.

Just for laughs:

Jean Peters and Samuel Fuller, left.

Thoughtful:

Moe and Skip, below.

Peters and Ritter, left.

Critic Bosley Crowther looked out his office window in the *New York Times* building to see that criminals were not nice people. "Violence bursts in every sequence, and the conversation is slangy and corrupt." – Crowther B. *'Pickup on South Street' Mixes Underworld Goons With Communist Spies*. June 18, 1953.

I am not sure what he meant by "corrupt" if it was not a synonym for "slangy". After thoroughly bagging the film, Crowther concludes with, "Sensations (Samuel Fuller) has in abundance and, in the delivery of them, Mr. Widmark, Miss Peters, Miss Ritter and all the others in the cast do very well." So, did Crowther like it? Who knows?

By 2015, Phillip French, in *The Guardian*, was far more empathetic with this "noir masterpiece".

"In one of her most moving performances of a blue-collar working woman Thelma Ritter was Oscar-nominated as a sympathetic stool pigeon who sells underworld information to the cops but refuses to betray the whereabouts of a fellow minor criminal to the communists."

French P. *Pickup on South Street – a masterly film noir. The Guardian*, 23 Aug 2015.

Thel & Sam

Sam Fuller was the writer/director of *Pickup on South Street,* and he gave Thelma Ritter juicy lines. Thel returned the compliment with delightfully wicked delivery. "If I was to be buried in Potter's Field, it would just about kill me." The movie is concerned with the class system or caste system, as Fuller called it in a 1989 interview for French television. "We have a caste system, snobs." – Schickel R. *Filmmakers of our Time.* 1989.

With the character of Moe, Fuller brilliantly exposes the nature of the caste system in a film that cancels the ruling caste out of the frame. There is an endearing quality to Moe's persistence in obtaining money for a burial plot, but also an understanding of the absurdity of dying to join the caste that excluded you all your life. "There'll be pie in the sky when I die," as the old folk song goes.

Fuller has an ambivalent attitude toward Moe's searching for deathly success as well as her profession. "Here's Thelma Ritter being a stool pigeon. Her job is stool pigeon." In the end, Fuller's begrudging judgment is the same as Skip's when he finds out Moe has sold his address. "Moe's all right. She's gotta eat."

Fuller's approach to his characters is different from the superficial analysis that the movie's theme is that the underclasses intuitively know that commies are bad. Remember Ritter says she just doesn't like commies, but she knows nothing about them. She is fodder for the demagogues such as Senator Joseph McCarthy and the members of the House Un-American Activities Committee.

Fuller was proud of pickpocket Skip, whom he described and visually displayed as an artist. Sure, Skip sneered at the authorities waving the flag at him. "Patriotism is the last refuge of a scoundrel," said Fuller, believing he was quoting one of his heroes, Benjamin Franklin. Like James Boswell, most attribute the bon mot to English lexicographer Samuel Johnson. No doubt Franklin, an icon of Fuller's 1952 film tribute to New York journalism *Park Row* 1952, would have strongly agreed with Johnson.

I am not a fan of much of Fuller's work. I find his lurid images coupled with bombastic music to be a parody of the best of noir. I can but shake my head at the start of his neo-noir *The Naked Kiss* 1964. Compare this to the beginning of Jules Dassin's 1948 noir *Naked City.*

No "The": It is *Naked City*, not The Naked City, except in France, where the movie becomes La *Cité Sans Voiles*.

I find few faults in *Pickup on South Street*. Richard Widmark's Skip is far more nuanced a criminal than his cackling psychopath Udo in *Kiss of Death* 1947 (still a good noir). In *Pickup on South Street,* Jean Peters gives a top performance as dull-witted Candy, used and abused by men who place her in jeopardy through schemes she does not understand. Thelma Ritter gives the finest performance of her career, which netted her six Oscar nominations. Shamefully, she did not win for *Pickup on South Street.*

From Here to Eternity cleaned up at the 26th Academy Awards held on March 25, 1954, simultaneously at the RKO Pantages Theatre, and NY's NBC Center Theatre (a cultural clash of name, Center in U.S. and Theatre in UK spelling). *From Here to Eternity* won best picture, directing (Fred Zinnemann) and supports (Frank Sinatra and Donna Reed). It was good to see noir stalwarts Reed and Zinnemann win gongs, but the film is a glorified soap opera.

Are you waving the flag at me.

The things they said

I'm so tired you'd be doing me a big favor if you blow my head off.

Waddya want from me? Do I personally raise the price of hamburgers? These are the prices.

More quotes

My first line was, "Don't wave the goddamn flag at me. So, Zanuck said, "Let's go soft on this, what the hell."

They removed only the "goddamn" which infuriated J. Edgar Hoover who wanted the whole line expunged. Zanuck refused. Fuller recalls Zanuck telling Hoover, "That's his (Skip's) character."

Fuller: (Skip) went after the man because he beat up his girl. He didn't go after the man for the United States or that phony Cold War stuff.

Candy: You've been recommended as the best pickpocket stoolie in the business.
Moe: What kind of talk is that, calling me a stoolie? I was brought up to report any injustice to the police authority. I call that being a solid citizen.
Candy: But you get paid for it.
Moe: You gonna knock it?

The Player

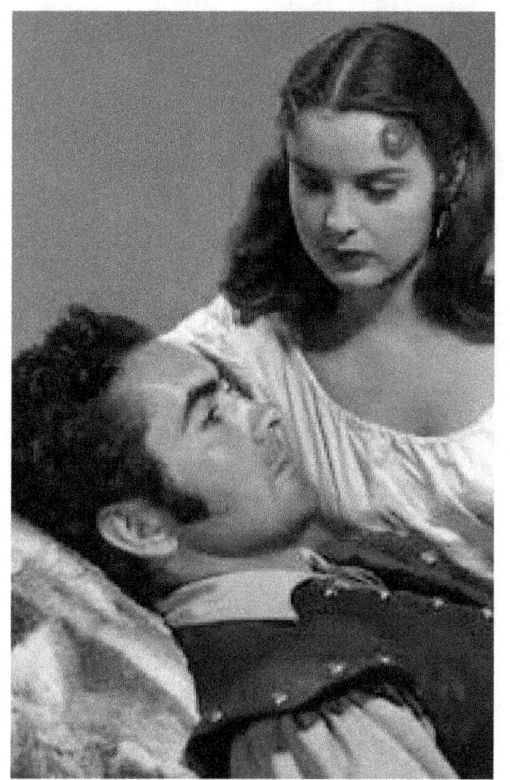

Jean Peters took little time to incur her first studio suspension. In her first film, *Captain from Castille* 1947, she played the love interest of swashbuckling heartthrob Tyrone Power. Fearful of typecasting, she refused the female lead in the Western *Yellow Sky* 1948. She told Fox the part was too sexy, and Fox told her she could sit on the sidelines without pay for a while. As Peters predicted, Anne Baxter's role in *Yellow Sky* was sexy.

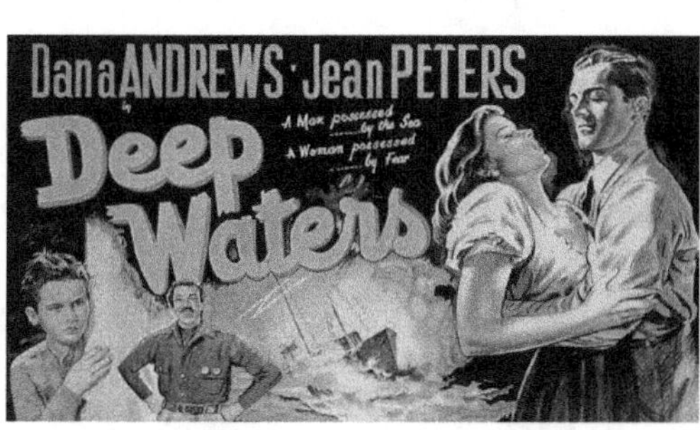

The studio and Peters compromised on her next movie *Deep Waters* 1948. Peters played a sensitive, sensible social worker, and Fox sexualized the misleading posters. A book on misleading posters is begging for an author, but not me.

Over the next seven years, Peters played in comedies, dramas, noirs, and Westerns with and without sexualized roles. Popular on the movie lots, Peters tired of fights with studio bosses and made her last film, the successful tear-jerker *A Man Called Peter* 1955. In 1957, she married Howard Hughes and stuck with him until 1971. Peters should have an Oscar for that.

Peters appeared with Joseph Cotten in *A Blueprint for Murder*, a plodding noir thriller that manages to be sordid and dull at the same time. It was a change of pace for Peters. She was competent enough to manage it, but writer/director Andrew Stone was not creative enough in either of his disciplines. Stone had a lengthy career in Hollywood, working on B-pictures. None of his movies stands out as a must-watch.

Vicki 1953 is a remake of the good 1941 noir *I Wake Up Screaming*. Someone should have screamed, "Too soon." The other point was that Carole Landis, who played Vicki in the original, suicided in 1948. A remake five years later strikes me as tacky. They changed Vicky to Vicki, maybe that was meant to trick us. Peters is good playing Vicki/Vicky, an attractive young woman, with natural charm.

Future prolific television producer Aaron Spelling plays Harry Williams, emulating the bit part memorably rendered by Elisha Cook Jr. in the 1941 iteration.

I must be psychic, I knew exactly how the plot would unfold.

Chapter 13

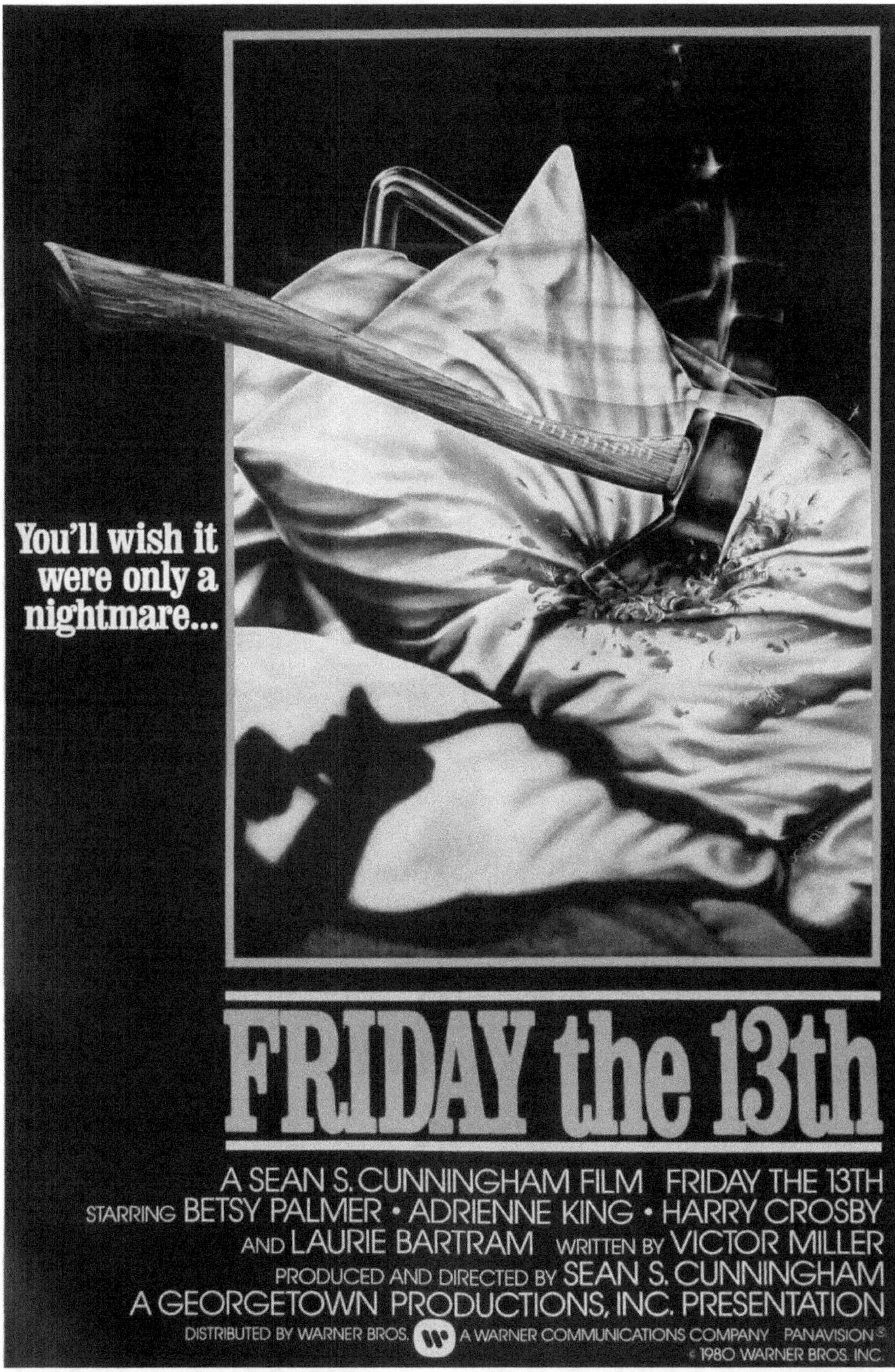

You'll wish it were only a nightmare...
FRIDAY the 13th
A SEAN S. CUNNINGHAM FILM FRIDAY THE 13TH
STARRING BETSY PALMER • ADRIENNE KING • HARRY CROSBY
AND LAURIE BARTRAM WRITTEN BY VICTOR MILLER
PRODUCED AND DIRECTED BY SEAN S. CUNNINGHAM
A GEORGETOWN PRODUCTIONS, INC. PRESENTATION
DISTRIBUTED BY WARNER BROS. A WARNER COMMUNICATIONS COMPANY PANAVISION®
© 1980 WARNER BROS. INC.

There is no Chapter 13

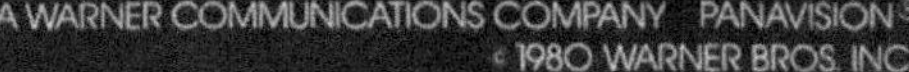

Chapter 14: Hitching a ride to suspense

Rear Window 1954, directed by Alfred Hitchcock, was a tremendous success at the box office, grossing more than twenty-five times its budget. But, over the years, discussions on the film have centred on its theme of voyeurism as a positive or negative social force. James Stewart plays a photographer with a broken leg. He becomes addicted to spying on his neighbours with binoculars and a camera. His nurse, Thelma Ritter, disapproves, "In the old days, they'd put your eyes out with a red-hot poker." She adds the cryptic assessment, "What people ought to do is get outside their own house and look in for a change." Thel is saying people should be more conscious of their aberrant behavior.

Because the protagonist is a male photographer, it is only logical that the movie explores cinema as shared voyeurism and the camera as a metaphor for the male gaze. What makes the discussion more salacious is Hitchcock's psycho-sexual sadism against blonde stars.

Blonde female lead Grace Kelly reported no harassment from Hitch, but the director placed her in sexualized poses.

The film has lashings of Hitchcock's trademark suspense and juvenile male humor.

John Michael Hayes wrote the Oscar-nominated script from a story by prolific noir writer Cornell Woolrich.

Stewart: He had something buried in that garden that the dog scented.

Wendell Corey: Like an old hambone?

Stewart: I don't know what pet names Thorwald had for his wife.

Funny, but passive-aggressive.

Hayes wrote another three films for Hitchcock: robbery romance *To Catch a Thief* 1955, the comedy, *The Trouble with Harry* 1955, and Hitchcock's remake of his own 1934 British film *The Man Who Knew Too Much* 1956.

What's in a name: Nova Pilbeam, the lead of the 1934 film, wasn't she named after an event in Olympic gymnastics?

I was happy to input my little jest, but that was the actor's birth name. Her parents were the Pilbeams, and her grandmother was from Nova Scotia.

The 1934 movie featured Hungarian Peter Lorre, who learned his English lines phonetically. In the remake, Doris Day sings the theme song *Que Será, Será (Whatever Will Be, Will Be)*, which could be an anthem of the fatalism of film noir. The 1956 version is a thriller, not a noir, while the 1934 version is a proto-noir. The movie posters give you an idea of the difference in styles and the lost art of poster making.

In D.H. Lawrence's 1927 novel *Lady Chatterley's Lover*, the husband's paralysis from the waist down is a symbol of his sexual impotence. Stewart's leg injury is also symbolic, but of his commitment phobia. Distinct reasons explain why this is a central theme. As a dramatic ploy, it makes the viewer think, "WTH is he doing, giving Grace Kelly the brush?" On behalf of the audience, Thel (Stella) expresses this view, "I can hear you now, 'Get out of my life, you wonderful woman. You're too good for me.'"

Stewart, on the other hand, gives the traditional " don't take my freedom " lament.

Stella: Maybe one day she'll find her happiness.

L.B. (Stewart): Yeah, some man'll lose his.

An adolescent male-centric view is that glamor model and magazine editor Lisa (Kelly) is too girly for the rigorous lifestyle of a globe-trotting photographer. Of course, it was inconceivable Lisa could be the major breadwinner and L.B. stay in the U.S. Unable to compete with her partner's voyeurism, Lisa helps solve the mystery. What a woman – eye candy and sex object, but basically, one of the boys.

Timely: At 26 minutes in, Alfred Hitchcock adjusts a clock in a songwriter's apartment. The time of certain happenings was crucial, we get that. But why is he adjusting the clock? Maybe the pianist is looking for inspiration for an arrangement of Bill Haley and the Comets' *Rock Around the Clock* 1954.

As well as Hayes' screenplay nomination, the Academy nominated Hitchcock for direction, Robert Burks for color cinematography, and Loren L. Ryder for sound.

Bob Hope hosted the 27th annual awards on March 30, 1955. Elia Kazan won direction for *On the Waterfront*, a shameless endorsement of the blacklisting by Senator Joseph McCarthy and the House Un-American Activities Committee.

Creatives never forgave formerly progressive theatrical director Kazan for naming names at the HUAC and following that up with the propaganda film *On the Waterfront*. At the 1999 Academy Awards, Martin Scorsese and Robert De Niro presented Kazan with a Lifetime Achievement Oscar. Actors Nick Nolte (*Cape Fear* 1991 with De Niro, directed by Scorsese), Ed Harris (*The Abyss* 1989), Susan Sarandon (*The Gutter* 2024), and Tim Robbins (*Dark Waters* 2019) sat grimly in their seats and refused to applaud.

George Seaton won screenplay for *The Country Girl*, for which Grace Kelly won best female actor. Best color photography went to Milton Krasner for *Three Coins in a Fountain*, and Leslie I. Carey won best sound for *The Glenn Miller Story*.

Chapter 15: Versatility is his long suit

Romanian-born director Jean Negulesco made his mark in 1940s' noir. *The Mark of Dimitrios* 1944, *Nobody Lives Forever* 1946, *and Road House* 1948 were three of his best, though others were popular. He also directed Jane Wyman in her Oscar-winning performance as a deaf-mute rape victim in *Johnny Belinda* 1948.

In the mid-1950s, Negulesco had hits with diverse films, the drama *Titanic* 1953, the comedy *How to Marry a Millionaire* 1953, the romantic comedy *Three Coins in a Fountain*, and the musical comedy *Daddy Long Legs* 1955. Thelma Ritter played in the first and last movies on that list.

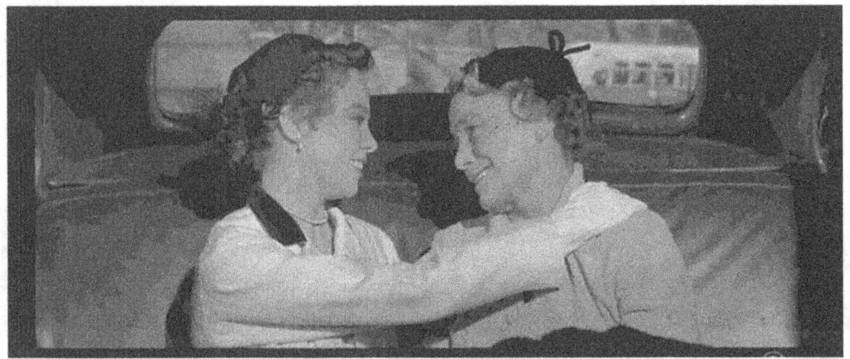

Les and Thel: Leslie Caron and Thelma Ritter in *Daddy Long Legs*.

This was the fourth Hollywood movie based on the 1912 novel by Jean Webster. Mary Pickford, above left, starred in *Daddy Long Legs* 1919. *Daddy Long Legs* 1931 starred Janet Gaynor, above middle. *Curly Top* 1935 starred Shirley Temple, above right.

The point of difference for the 1955 version was that it was a musical. Fred Astaire, in his mid-fifties, could still cavort to the beat. His long-time partner Ginger Rogers put away her dancing shoes before she turned thirty. Her last movie was *The Story of Vernon and Irene Castle* 1939, but Rogers returned a decade later to replace an ill Judy Garland in *The Barkleys of Broadway*. *New York Times* critic Bosley Crowther delicately compared their tenth picture to the other nine. "Maybe they're favoring slightly their educated legs in this most felicitous reunion." Crowther B. *Ginger Rogers and Fred Astaire Teamed Again in 'Barkleys of Broadway,' at State*, May 5, 1949.

In reviewing the 1955 iteration of *Daddy Long Legs*, *NYT* critic Abraham H. Weiler showed he could convolute prose as maladroitly as Crowther. "Even an indulgent observer can note that "Daddy Long Legs" is a fragile and attenuated fiction."
– Weiler A.H. *'Daddy Long Legs'; Old Story, New Dances* May 6, 1955, page 18.
Weiler commented on the acting talent who aggrandized the attenuated moving picture (I am practicing being a film critic in New York).
"Fred Clark does a neat and professional stint as Mr. Astaire's harried right-hand man; Thelma Ritter is equally competent as his testy secretary, and Terry Moore makes a pretty picture in her few, brief appearances as Mr. Astaire's niece and Miss Caron's college roommate."

Terry Moore, aged 97 at the time of publication of this book, was a popular actor in the 1940s and 1950s before transitioning into television in the 1960s. She was in the film noirs *Gaslight* 1944, *Shadowed* 1946, *Gambling House* 1951, and *Two of a Kind* 1951, before being nominated for best support for the drama *Come Back Little Sheba* 1952. The female lead was Broadway actor Shirley Booth. In her first screen role, Booth took the Oscar for her part as an unhappily married woman, reliving past traumas in judgmental 1950s America.

Sentimental craftsman and the winner of four directing Oscars Frank Capra emerged from six years of making educational films to direct *A Hole in the Head* 1959. The strong cast included Frank Sinatra, Edward G. Robinson, Eleanor Parker, Carolyn Jones, Keenan Wynn, and Thelma Ritter.

Capra tells how Ritter approached him with reverse psychology after Sinatra's low boredom threshold threatened to derail the movie. Sinatra disliked multiple rehearsals and takes. The director figured Sinatra was like Barbara Stanwyck – a performer, not an actor. Edward G. Robinson was the opposite – rehearse, rehearse, rehearse until it was right. The veteran actor figured Sinatra was dissing him by refusing to rehearse with him. Then comes the intervention by Ritter ("that best of all character actors", according to Capra). "Told you Robinson was going to stink. I'm gonna stink, Sinatra's gonna stink, you're gonna stink, and the picture's gonna stink." Capra F, 1971, page 459.

Capra writes that Ritter repeated the litany of "stinks", and he implies she was taking advantage of the reversed power relationship between directors and actors after actor-heavy independent companies replaced studios. Ritter's colleagues never reported her as being vindictive, and it was more likely Ritter's warning to Capra to sort out the dispute. Sinatra's company owned two-thirds of *A Hole in the Head,* and the director owned the other third. Capra insisted that Robinson rehearse with a stand-in and added to Robinson's agent that he would sue if the actor bailed. In parts of his autobiography, the Italian American Capra talks like a Mafioso. And he reacted badly to the diminished authority of a director.

Capra diplomatically declared to cast and crew that Robinson was the best actor in the world, and the set broke out in applause. Sinatra walked in to see all the respect, and Robinson rushed over to Sinatra to pinch his cheeks.

Capra maintained Ritter continued to needle him and that her movie "get your goat" humor extended off the set. He exudes sarcasm, describing Ritter thanking him after the successful preview. "A tear-stained face clamped onto mine . . . Oh Frank . . . It's so wonderful . . . I'm so proud to be a part of it . . . so proud." Capra F. 1971, page 460.

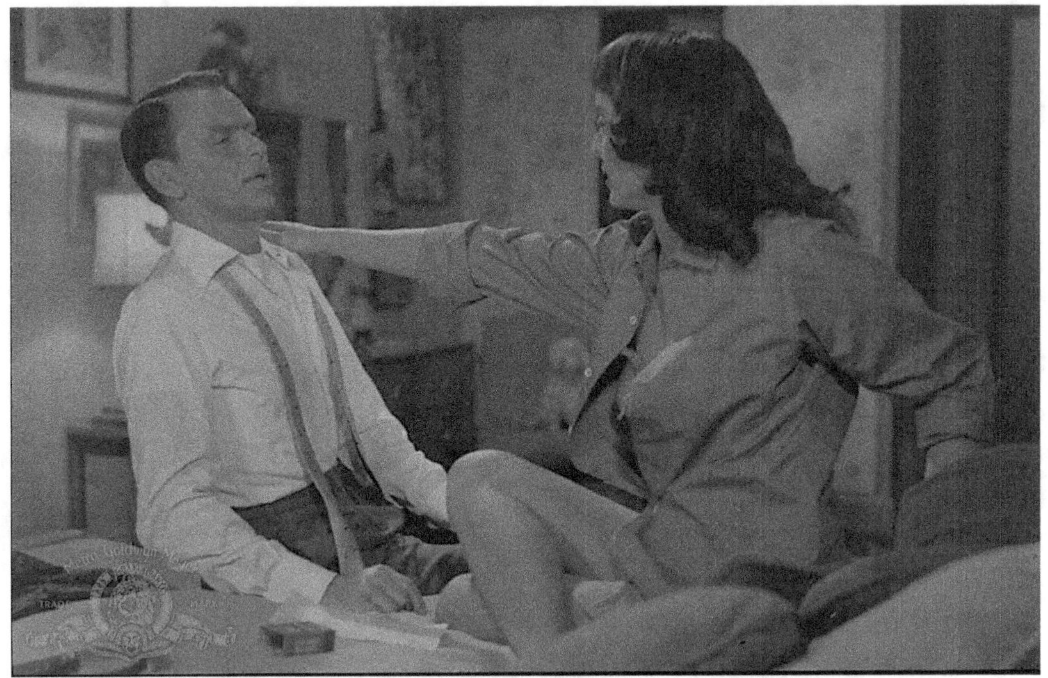

The humor and social manners of *A Hole in the Head* are dated. Women are broads, says Sinatra, talking to his 12-year-old son, and Parker keeps martinis at hand in the icebox. Carolyn Jones, the future Morticia Addams of the ghoulish television family, played a beatnik transitioning into a hippie, and she provided the best parts of the film. Jones disappeared at the end of the second act, and with her went the frivolity.

Capra changed the central family's ethnicity to Italian, but the cadence and content of the Jewish jests from screenwriter Arnold Schulman's Broadway play remain.

The sentimentality of the closing scenes would have had viewers feeling good as they left the cinema. It was well-constructed pathos, but inconsistent with what transpired before, and offered a sugar hit instead of intellectual nourishment.

Thelma Ritter bounces between being mean to hubby, Edward G. Robinson, and being sympathetic to the woes of other characters. There is little depth to the stereotypes of stingy hubby and weepy wife. Dedicated Ritter and Robinson do best as they can with the material.

Chapter 17: A Rocky Date

Pillow Talk 1959 was the first of three romcoms pairing Rock Hudson and Doris Day — the beefcake meets the babe next door. Why the young woman next door was always prim and proper and never sensual was an enduring mystery throughout the 1950s. But there she was, prim and proper, down to the name Doris. The yin and yang of it was that Doris had a sassy housekeeper, Thelma Ritter, sweeping up another Oscar nomination, number 5, if you are counting.

It is a feat for director Michael Gordon (noirs *The Web* 1947, *An Act of Murder* 1948, and *Woman in Hiding* 1949) and cinematographer Arthur E. Arling (camera operator, *Gone with the Wind* 1939) to build a solid comic structure around the slight framework of a shared "party" telephone line before individual telephony was rolled out.

Pillow Talk is a pleasant comedy once you come to terms with the concepts that alcoholic Ritter (To the elevator operator: "Must you zoom up so fast?") and playboy predator Hudson ("six dates oughta do it") play funny stereotypes. The sexual innuendo is unsophisticated, but Day and Hudson deliver funny lines with a light touch. Split screens and conflicting interior monologues work well. Hudson's affectation of a good ol' boy from Texas is appealing. The forays into slapstick, such as Hudson trying to squeeze into a Citroen roadster, are unexpected delights.

Costume designer Jean Louis designed the array of chic clothing Day wore. Louis had designed for the noirs *Gilda* 1945, *The Lady from Shanghai* 1948, *The Big Heat* 1953, and *Queen Bee* 1955.

After a decade in movies, Ritter may have been Oscar-nominated for her body of work. In *Pillow Talk,* she brought nothing to the table that cried out, exceptional work.

Ritter's funniest line is in response to a suggestion that a single career woman is missing something important.

Day: What's a girl supposed to do? Go out on the street, and ask the first man she meets to come home with her?

Ritter: No - don't do that, ma'am. (Pause) It don't work.

So, it is not a comedic gem, but neither is Thelma's part.

Closeted gay actor Hudson pretends to be a Texan (quite a convincing accent, too) to seduce Day. There is something weird about the scene where Hudson, whom Day has never seen, tries to manipulate her into having sex with his Texan alter ego.

Hudson: That's even worse than I thought.

Day: Worse? What do you mean worse?

Hudson: Oh well, must I spell it out? Either you're not telling the truth or . . .

Day: Or what?

Hudson: Well, there are some men who just – well, they're very devoted to their mothers. The type that likes to collect cooking recipes or exchange bits of gossip.

Day: What a vicious thing to say.

What a homophobic scene in a movie that won the Oscar for best original screenplay (Story from social issues filmmakers Russell Rouse and Clarence Greene; screenplay: Stanley Shapiro and Maurice Richlin).

Rock Hudson died from AIDS-related complications in 1985. After the death of her co-star and friend, Doris Day became actively engaged in HIV/AIDS awareness and fundraising.

The Canadian magazine *Gay Globe* recognized her contributions with a cover story of Day in issue #79, October 29, 2011. The cover photo is from the 1950s. October 2 was the date in 1985 that Hudson died.

In a 2015 interview with *People Magazine* Day said, "The reason people liked our movies is because they could tell how much we liked each other."

It was good to see two familiar noir faces in the supporting cast. Playing an elevator operator was proto-noir regular Allen Jenkins (*Dead End* 1937, *Racket Busters* 1938, and *The Amazing Dr. Clitterhouse* 1938). Playing a rich tasteless southern matron was noir stalwart Lee Patrick (Effie, *The Maltese Falcon* 1941, *Mildred Pierce* 1945, *The Snake Pit* 1948, *Caged* 1949, and *The Lawless* 1950).

Playing Patrick's son was Nick Adams (*Rebel Without a Cause* 1955, *and* pictured right as the lead in the ABC television show *The Rebel* 1959-61, and Oscar nominee for the courtroom drama *Twilight of Honor* 1963.

Adams starred in two Japanese monster films that have become cult favorites *Frankenstein vs. Baragon* 1965 and *Invasion of Astro-Monster* 1965.

To Oscar or not to Oscar

Thelma Ritter received a nom for best support for *Pillow Talk*. Doris Day was among the nominees for best female actor at the 32nd Academy Awards, along with:

Simone Signoret

Elizabeth Taylor/ Katharine Hepburn

Audrey Hepburn

First, that nun is in dubious company. Second, I do not get a film's dual nominations in the same category. In *Suddenly Last Summer*, Elizabeth Taylor was the lead, ahead of Katharine Hepburn and Montgomery Clift. Signoret won the award.

Remember what happened with *All About Eve*. The Academy nominated Bette Davis and Anne Baxter for best actor. Neither won. Davis was clearly the female lead, and the title itself was a jest, as the movie was all about Margo. Thelma Ritter and Celeste Holm were nominated for best support. Josephine Hull deserved her win for the comedy drama *Harvey*, but dual nominations did not improve Ritter's or Holm's chances.

Actors have won from dual nominations. Curiously, Meryl Streep, who was the female lead, won best support for *Kramer vs. Kramer* 1979. Streep's co-nominee from *Kramer vs. Kramer* for best support, Jane Alexander, was in a weak field, apart from Streep. On the other hand, Sally Field beat a strong field for best actor. Streep's nomination for best support seemed a product of horse trading to cynical ol' me.

Best Actress in a Leading Role

Sally Field – *Norma Rae* as Norma Rae Webster‡

- Jill Clayburgh – *Starting Over* as Marilyn Holmberg
- Jane Fonda – *The China Syndrome* as Kimberly Wells
- Marsha Mason – *Chapter Two* as Jennie MacLaine
- Bette Midler – *The Rose* as Mary Rose "The Rose" Foster

Best Actress in a Supporting Role

- Meryl Streep – *Kramer vs. Kramer* as Joanna Kramer‡
  - Jane Alexander – *Kramer vs. Kramer* as Margaret Phelps
  - Barbara Barrie – *Breaking Away* as Evelyn Stohler
  - Candice Bergen – *Starting Over* as Jessica Potter
  - Mariel Hemingway – *Manhattan* as Tracy

The movie billing above is clear: Dustin Hoffman bills above Meryl Streep, who, as the female lead, bills ahead of the third lead, Jane Alexander.

Chapter 18: Back in noir

Thelma Ritter and Marilyn Monroe had memorable parts in the 1950 noir satire *All About Eve*. A decade later, they reunited for an unusual film with the potential for greatness. It was a neo-noir neo-Western romance with the bleak title *The Misfits* 1961. Hauling a wagon full of Oscars, Tonys, and a Pulitzer were director John Huston, actor Clark Gable, cinematographer Russell Metty, and screenwriter Arthur Miller.

In the noir tradition, problems erupted on location in a sweltering Nevada desert. The marriage of Arthur Miller and Marilyn Monroe was melting. Macho Clark Gable, 59, insisted on doing his own stunts, though director Huston vetoed the veteran actor doing the more dangerous ones. Gable died from a heart attack two days after filming finished. Monroe, 36, died two years later from a declared suicide, though the inevitable conspiracy theories raged about her "murder". In 1966, Montgomery Clift, 45, died from a heart attack after years of dependence on alcohol and medications. Ritter, born a year after Gable, was sixty-six when she died in early 1969. If only they had called that movie *The Happy-Go-Luckies*.

Despite the setbacks, *The Misfits* turned out to be a good movie, hurt by mediocre reviews, but critically rehabilitated later.

Three amigos: Thel, Marilyn, and Gable.

Despite Monroe inconveniencing everyone, Ritter and she had a good relationship on location in Nevada. Monroe had a habit of giving gifts to people she had offended or were kind to her. Bonhams auction house sold this letter with a Christmas card from Ritter to Monroe for USD360 in June 2007. John Huston told of another Monroe giftee: "When we talked about Marilyn, tears came to Suzanne's eyes. She knew somehow — we all did — that something awful was going to happen to her."

Huston J. *An Open Book,* Virgin Books, London 1994, page 289.

Thelma Ritter

August 29, 1960

Dear "Millie" Monroe:

I no sooner opened the box than that damned lizard escaped.

I spent all day looking for him, and finally found him under the refrigerator with the quarter in his mouth making like a slot machine.

Incidentally, the bag is beautiful. And I thank you very much. But it doesn't take you off the hook with regard to the "honor system".

Big Brother is watching you.

Keep your eye on Paula, May, Hazel, Agnes, and Shirley.

Every country has a place to run away to, from a busted relationship, a bankruptcy, or a crime. In Australia, the place to run to was Darwin. My apologies to Darwinians if I speak out of school, and that is no longer the case. In America, it was Nevada to where people ran for easy divorces and fast money in the casinos. In film noir and in real life. In a great early scene in *The Misfits*, Isabelle (Thelma Ritter) expounds on leaving things behind in Nevada.

Isabelle: I even left my southern accent here . . . I wasn't beautiful enough to go back home. Beauty's a help any place, but (southern accent) in Virginia, it's a necessity. We can't hardly get a driver's license without it."

Ritter, arm in cast, plays a landlady who rents rooms to travelling divorcées. Ritter brightly delivers Miller's sparkling dialogue, "I'm all set, I just ironed the sleeve (holding her cast) . . . At my last roomer's, we celebrated her divorce, and I misbehaved. (Ritter turns on a dime to show the darker side of her personality). I'm so sick and tired of myself."

This scene is an unusual but pleasant start to a Hollywood movie that underwhelmed critics at its debut but delighted later appraisers.

When Monroe nervously practices for her divorce hearing, we suspect her husband Miller is about to unleash a partial biography of his wife, who was notoriously nervous before performances she had thoroughly learned the lines for. Jean Louis designed Miss Monroe's wardrobe.

Miller had written *The Misfits* after his quickie divorce in Reno, Nevada, in 1956, before his registry office marriage to Monroe less than three weeks later. In 1959, Miller sent the first script to Huston with a note that the female lead was meant for Monroe. That script included characters based on people Miller met in Nevada.
– Hannan B. *Behind the Scenes: The Misfits*, in *themagnificent60s.com*.

Mutual admiration: Huston, Monroe, and Miller.

Monroe and Miller recalled director Huston helping Monroe overcome nerves to deliver a career breakout role in *The Asphalt Jungle,* as I recounted in a previous book.
– Dowling B. *Man Of A Thousand Fails*, Bent Banana Books, 2016, page 97.
"That role was the beginning for Marilyn, and she was always grateful to me," Huston wrote. "It led – a decade later – to our working together in *The Misfits,* her last completed film." – Huston J. 1994, page 287.

Monroe caused cost blowouts with her lateness and two-week stay in hospital, but she turned in a superior performance.

An adjustment Monroe made to ameliorate nervousness was her bringing an acting coach – usually from the theater – to her films. For *The Asphalt Jungle* it was German émigré Natasha Lytess, pictured right. Paula Strasberg was on $3000 a week for *The Misfits,* and she could and did demand additional takes from Huston. That security blanket would not have improved Monroe's confidence or the temper of directors.

Animal lover: In this powerful climactic scene, Monroe screams at the three freedom-loving men, taking away the freedom of wild horses.

It was disappointing to see Ritter written out of the picture before the start of the third act. The bonding of Marilyn and Thelma in their reaction to the Nevada cowboys was a theme of the picture. But Miller wanted to take a different tack to explore Gable, Clift, and Eli Wallach's love or lust for Monroe. This theme is set against their desperate attempts to retain a disappearing lifestyle, just like the few remaining mustangs they want to capture to sell for pet food. Monroe, haunted by abandonment as a child, cannot bear to see men or beasts in pain.

This is Monroe's film, though Gable received top billing. She is excellent and is an example of the strange profession of acting in which alcoholics and drug addicts can turn in fine work. That is not to say their work would not have been better if they had kicked the alcohol and pills.

Monroe acts superbly in one subversive scene. Gable posts photos of her on a locker's inside door. An embarrassed Monroe tries to close the door, but a voyeuristic Wallach wants to look. The photos are obviously studio publicity shots that recreated a shy young Monroe as a siren. Brilliant scene.

Biopic *Birdman of Alcatraz* is loose with the truth, but it is an uplifting story of redemption through altruism and intellectual curiosity. Thelma Ritter, as the Birdman's mother, flew home empty handed after her sixth Oscar nomination.

I do prefer veracity in a biopic, but when you see the narrator Edmond O'Brien pretending to be Birdman biographer Thomas E. Gaddis, you know entertainment is privileged over accuracy.

Noir old timers: Karl Malden, Neville Brand, and Burt Lancaster.

It was good to see a couple of noir veterans turn in clever work in *Birdman of Alcatraz*. Karl Malden (*Kiss of Death* 1948, *Where the Sidewalk Ends* 1950, *I Confess* 1953) adds nuance to the Hollywood stereotype of the harsh warden. Malden had a rare ability to convey paradoxical quiet earnestness to make his characters compelling. A memorable role was a minor one as a spurned suitor in *A Streetcar Named Desire* 1951. Brand, who plays a gruff guard of Birdman Robert Stroud, turned in two remarkable villainous performances in the noirs *D.O.A.* 1950 and *Kansas City Confidential* 1952. Lancaster appeared in noir classics such as *The Killers* 1946, *Sorry, Wrong Number* 1948, *Criss Cross* 1949, *Sweet Smell of Success* 1957, and the neo-noir *Elmer Gantry* 1960.

In a powerful scene, Brand explodes when the unsociable Lancaster asks for the wooden box the screw is sitting on. Brand admonishes Lancaster for never speaking to him casually during the past 12 years and says he would not give him the box for $100. Lancaster apologizes sincerely. Then we see the scene above with only Brand's hands and feet within noir lighting as he puts the box in the cell. A filmmaker mines gold with a small but moving scene like that.

Good line

Lancaster tells Brand there will be new life in his cell as his two canaries are mating.
Brand: I guess they won't mind, canaries are always behind bars, anyway. (to mix species, Brand was speaking about stool pigeons, aka canaries).

Oscar-nominated for best support, Telly Savalas became a godfather to the first canary born in the Birdman's cell. He became a television icon as the lollipop-sucking detective *Kojak, 1973-78*, and reprised the role in seven telemovies in the 1980s.

Hollywood movie makers, creating in the most psychoanalyzed country on earth, still loved their Freud in the early 1960s. The rift between mother and son was historically accurate. It happened after the Birdman and widow Stella Johnson (Betty Field, pictured above right as Johnson, who was Della Mae Jones in real life) became partners in bird medicines. Romance ensued, though Robert Stroud never left prison.

Thelma to Lancaster: "It will be just like the old days, just the two of us together."

Robert Stroud refused to annul his marriage to Stella Johnson and Elizabeth McCartney Stroud refused to campaign for her son's parole.

In the film, Thelma Ritter says to a reporter, "My son is where he belongs." After 1933, Elizabeth Stroud never spoke to her son again. She left Leavenworth and died in 1938.

Me or her: "Give her up, Robbie. Forget her."

The Shooter

The cinematography of Burnett Guffey is superb and quite remarkable, given the physical confines of shots.

Guffey was a prolific shooter of film noirs, mostly B-pictures. Citing examples comes down to choosing favorites rather than estimating the best. My favorites are *Framed* 1947, *All the King's Men* 1949, *In a Lonely Place* 1950, *The Sniper* 1952, and *Human Desire* 1954.

Guffey's two Oscars were for *From Here to Eternity* 1953 and the gangster biopic *Bonnie and Clyde* 1967.

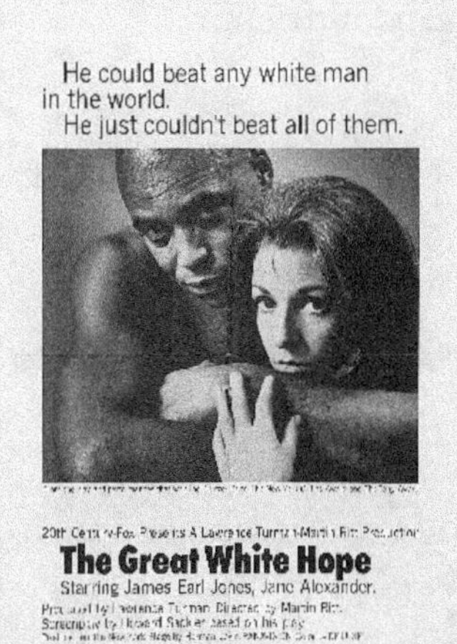

One of Guffey's last films was the retro boxing biopic The *Great White Hope* 1970, about the career of Jack Johnson who was the first Black heavyweight champion, after he defeated Tommy Burns in Sydney, Australia, in 1908. The movie title refers to calls for a Great White Hope to take the title from Johnson.

Like the Birdman, Johnson, the nemesis of The Great White Hope, spent time in Leavenworth, one year and one day, for violating the Mann Act, by taking a woman across state lines for immoral purposes.

Combatants: James Gandolfini confronts Robert Redford in *The Last Castle* 2001.

In these socially polarized days, people will fight over anything. People savage *Birdman of Alcatraz* for the inaccuracy of its title. Yet the film does not claim Stroud kept birds after his transfer to Alcatraz Island prison, which banned pets. Also, the title was the same as the book on which the film was based. Moreover, a movie called The Birdman of Leavenworth would have created false expectations of it being about the military prison, which is the setting for the film *The Last Castle*.

By the time the book appeared, people had read or heard about the military prison of Leavenworth. It was not the same jail that incarcerated Robert Stroud. The United States Military Barracks is a prison in Fort Leavenworth. It has always been known colloquially as Leavenworth. People outside of the State of Kansas confuse it with the nearby Leavenworth Federal Penitentiary.

Complaints that Lancaster subdued the personality of the angry and aggressive Stroud are more valid. Lancaster plays him as a quiet, emotionally distant prisoner. In real life, guards and inmates referred to him as manipulative, violent, and unfriendly.

Criticisms of Stroud's scientific work are less valid. I read unscientific accusations that Stroud's bird medicine was found to be ineffective. But I found no professional debunking of the value of his work.

The film tends to emphasize Stroud's experimentation in discovering cures for avian diseases, but he was a voracious reader with an IQ between 112 and 116. Stroud was a self-taught scientist who worked for years in an underexplored discipline.

24 GREAT STARS IN THE MIGHTIEST ADVENTURE EVER FILMED!
METRO·GOLDWYN·MAYER
and
CINERAMA
present
HOW THE WEST WAS WON
STARRING
CARROLL BAKER · LEE J. COBB · HENRY FONDA · CAROLYN JONES
KARL MALDEN · GREGORY PECK · GEORGE PEPPARD
ROBERT PRESTON · DEBBIE REYNOLDS · JAMES STEWART
ELI WALLACH · JOHN WAYNE · RICHARD WIDMARK · NARRATED BY SPENCER TRACY
METROCOLOR
THE TINHORN
THE FARM GIRL
BUFFALO HUNTER
GAMBLER'S BRIDE
MOUNTAIN MAN
THE SOD BUSTER
HORSE SOLDIER
WAGON MASTER
FRONTIER MARSHAL
MARSHAL'S WIFE
THE DESPERADO
THE GENERAL
EMPIRE BUILDER
CO-STARRING
BRIGID BAZLEN · WALTER BRENNAN · DAVID BRIAN · ANDY DEVINE · RAYMOND MASSEY · AGNES MOOREHEAD · HENRY (HARRY) MORGAN
THELMA RITTER · MICKEY SHAUGHNESSY · RUSS TAMBLYN · WRITTEN BY JAMES R. WEBB · DIRECTED BY HENRY HATHAWAY, JOHN FORD, GEORGE MARSHALL
PRODUCED BY BERNARD SMITH · MUSIC BY ALFRED NEWMAN

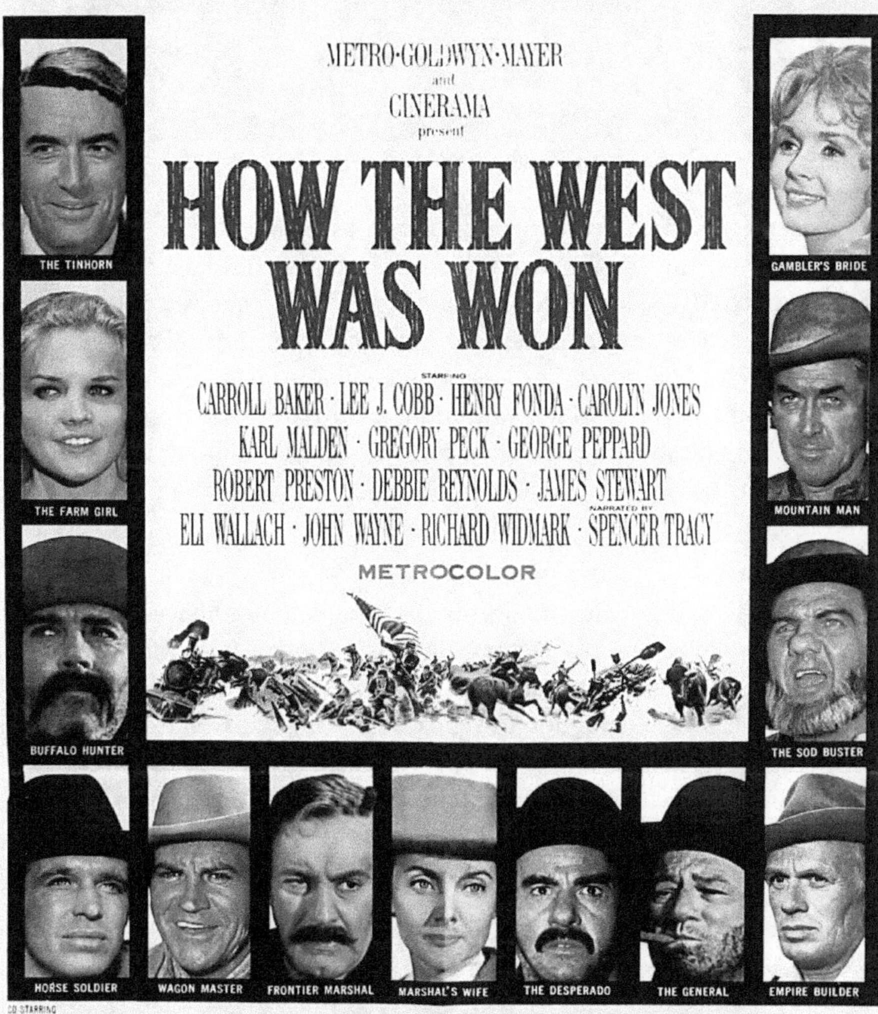

1962

How the West Was Won was a big gamble with 24 A-list actors, three directors, and four cinematographers running up a tab of twelve million before-blockbuster (BB) dollars. The gamble paid off when the epic anthology Western grossed $50 million at the box office. That is more than half a billion dollars in 2026 values, not to be sneezed at, even in after-blockbuster (AB) currency.

Rob & Thel: Robert Preston and Thelma Ritter.

Filming in Cinerama involved attaching three cameras to give significant width. Technical issues were the inability to do close-ups, unsynced sound, and actors' eyelines not matching. Extras filled lavish sets. Cinemas needed expensive conversions to show the three-camera process, which lasted for only one other film, *The Wonderful World of the Brothers Grimm*, a box-office loser despite being one of the highest grossers of 1962. The epic comedy *It's a Mad, Mad, Mad, Mad World* 1963 grossed $60 million. Advertised as photographed in Cinerama, cinematographers shot it in single-lens Ultra Panavision 70. Three-camera technology designed to awe audiences and drag them away from their television sets proved a lasting success in its less expensive second-generation product.

Technical flaws detracted from the drama, but the setup enhanced the visuals. This showed at the Academy Awards. Actors, directors Henry Hathaway, John Ford, and George Marshall; and cinematographers William Daniels, Milton Krasner, Charles Lang, and Joseph LaShelle won not a single Oscar. The film won Academy Awards for original screenplay (James R. Webb, a lucky win), editing (Howard F. Kress) and sound (Franklin Milton). The latter two earned their Oscars by fixing the bugs of Cinerama.

Spectacular:
The Wonderful World of the Brothers Grim gave grandeur to a curved screen.

How the West Was Won had five narratives, three directed by Hathaway, and one each by Ford and Marshall, who had been directing Westerns way back to 1916. Marshall directed the classic noir *The Blue Dahlia* 1946. He is below, left, with Marlene Dietrich and producer Joe Pasternak at the Universal cafeteria during the production of *Destry Rides Again* 1939. Dietrich was glamorous, but the eatery was far from flash. Marshall directed so many movies and television shows that you will have to count them yourself. I have a book to finish.

Starting a 2-hour 44-minute film with a 4-minute 25-second overture might not have been the smartest strategy. Still, the producer Bernard Smith (former literary editor of Raymond Chandler and Dashiell Hammett) and musical director Alfred Newman got away with it. The image, top left, of a stagecoach guard shooting at a Native American is on-screen for the first seven minutes.

Narrator Spencer Tracy tells us the western United States had to be won. From Nature. And Primitive Man.

A favorite noir villain, Lee Van Cleef, makes an uncredited appearance as, you guessed it, a baddie. Another noir and dramatic fave, Agnes Moorehead, appeals as the level-headed wife and mother constraining her exuberant family, Karl Malden, Carroll Baker, and Debbie Reynolds.

Debbie Reynolds is the link between the first segment *The Rivers* and the second *The Plains*. She hitches a ride on Ritter's wagon, bound for California. Thelma is after a husband. She figures Reynolds is good man bait.

Thelma Ritter's character is a familiar one, a straight-talking woman with a softer side. Cinema goers loved the persona. So did astute filmmakers who wanted to enliven the dull moments that invade every film. If Thel made it to California, she might not find another useless hubby, but she would get work.

Resistance: The "primitive men" arrive to defend their land.

Love at last: Thel gets her man on a riverboat.

John Ford's *Civil War* segment was the shortest and least effective. It looked like he spent so much money on the short battle scenes, full of sound and fury, that he had little left for drama. Telling instead of showing went on, including about the deaths of two major characters from *The Rivers*. Generals Sherman and Grant (John Wayne and Harry Morgan) had a post-mortem about the day's battle and exchanged vague musings on competence.

The Railroad segment, directed by George Marshall, showed how to make a movie with 12, 000 bit-players and extras to take full advantage of the wide screen. The scene above looked great for fifteen expensive seconds.

Native Americans stampeding buffalo onto the railroad invaders was an epic scene. Director Marshall must have sweet-talked producer Bernard Smith into opening the purse strings. The scene used up to 1200 buffalo, controlled by stunt riders and cowboys, after Native Americans refused to take part in the scene. Cinematographer Joseph LaShelle said there were two hundred buffalo, but he added they were running ninety abreast, which would only make two rows. – *American Cinematographer* magazine, October 1983. Two hundred seems fewer than those on the screen, while ninety abreast seems an exaggeration.

Director Henry Hathaway was supposed to direct only one of the five segments but did three. He was then critical of his co-directors. "(I) did over the fourth one, the railroad-building sequence of Marshall's. It was awful. The only one I didn't do over was Ford's — and I should have, because it was lousy. But I didn't want it known in the industry that I was doing over John Ford's work!"
– *American Cinematographer* magazine, October 1983.
I wonder why Hollywood disparaged Hathaway for his ego.

"I guess I'm not an Indian (Native American)," says George Peppard. "A man belongs with his own kind, like 'em or not."
Sounds like a cryptic version of white supremacy. Peppard left the mountain to ride into "civilization".

Peppard became a U. S. marshal, married the fabulous Carolyn Jones, and raised a family. Life was perfect until he had to front gunslinger Eli Wallach, whose brother Peppard had killed. When Wallach heard there would be no close-ups, he decided to overact so that his character Charlie Gant would spill across the whole wide screen.

How the West Was Won is an attractive film, even on a television screen or a computer monitor. But it lacks intellectual depth, and drama. As the wise woman said, all that glitters . . .

Chapter 21: Ride a train into the last noir

Thelma Ritter's second-to-last film, the neo-noir *The Incident* 1967, depicts the relationships of passengers boarding a train at the Bronx stations. They are a diverse lot, but all seem overwhelmed by angst. Martin Sheen, in his first film role, and Tony Musante are two New York punks who menace passengers trapped on the subway train.

Out of Brooklyn: Thelma travels through the Bronx, and this happens.

The most memorable aspect of this movie is the May-and-December mix of young bloods and veteran performers. Beau Bridges was in his first key role, and Donna Mills was making her debut. Beside Ritter, in the December group, was Jack Gilford as her husband. Co-passengers were Gary Merrill, Jan Sterling, Ruby Dee, and Brock Peters. Ed McMahon, who pioneered the essential role of talk-show-host Offsider alongside Johnny Carson, was on board.

The film is something of a potboiler early, but it was good to see a rudimentary peace sign on the subway wall, to our left of Donna Mills' right hand. I have pondered how Americans must watch their movies differently from overseas denizens who do not recognize the geography and structures.

Recent reviews of film noirs will sometimes write about destroyed or repurposed buildings of Los Angeles, San Francisco, Chicago, and New York.

Thelma had an angry husband in *As Young as You Feel*, an angrier one in *A Hole in the Head* and the angriest of all in *The Incident*. He is annoyed with their son, who "has a good job" but will not give his dad $500 for dental work. We get the impression hubby is mad at the world, in general.

It takes half the screen time to explain the conflicts the passengers are dragging on to the train, and viewers are feeling the deadweight of the preamble before the thrills begin. Forceful dizzying cinematography by Gerald Hirschfeld (noir *C-Man* 1949, comedy drama *Goodbye Columbus* 1969, spoof *Young Frankenstein* 1974) captures the arrival of the two punks into the train carriage. The movie rises from its slumber.

Everything rises – the acting, the terse dialog, and the close photography. The film morphs into a claustrophobic noir that it should have been much earlier, when it lost its way and privileged telling over showing.

Gilford and Ritter deliver top-shelf acting as the elderly man turns out to be the bravest in the carriage when the two young punks become substitutes for his ungrateful son. Ritter is fearful for her husband's life. This train is the right vehicle for two veteran actors to draw upon their years of experience.

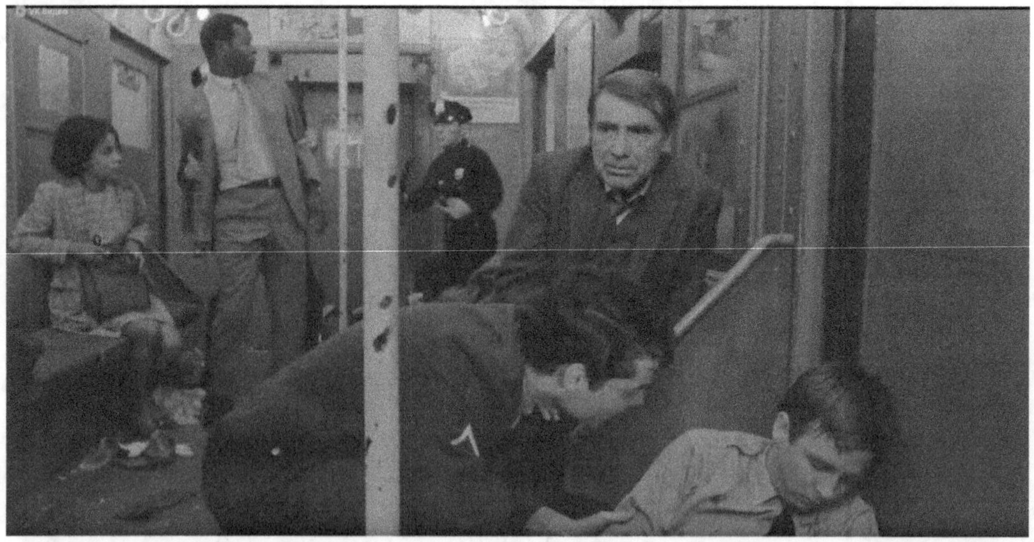

In a shocking scene, the police arrive in the carriage and wrongly assume who has committed the carnage.

This is a great film from 50-minutes in.

If you enjoyed my book, you might like to leave a review or rating on Amazon Books or at your favorite bookstore – Bernie.

Enjoyed *TY, Thel*.

Dive deeper into the shadows of classic Hollywood with my other books.

Discover the **Photo-Rich Series**:

- ***Noir Dirt Cheap***
- ***Film Noir Fate Vs The Working Stiff***
- ***Starry Starry Noir Rebels And Censors***
- ***Three Faces of Noir Curse Crime Cringe***

Enjoy my photo-rich affordable series

Classic Hollywood Snapshots

- ***TY, Thel***
- ***Man of a Thousand Fails***
- ***Volume III*** is coming soon

Selected bibliography

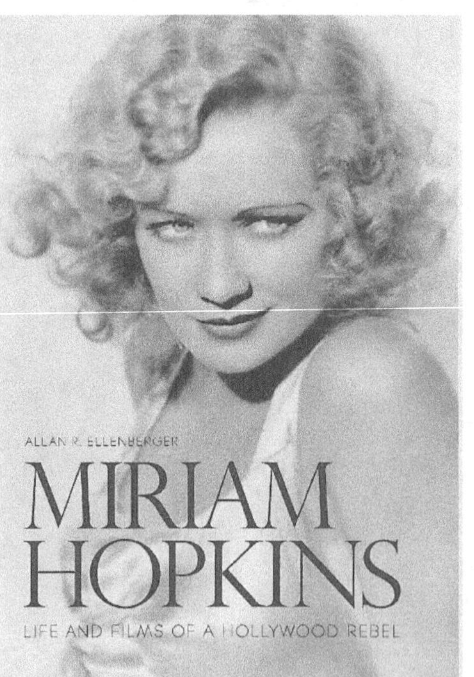

$2.50
American
Cinematographer
INTERNATIONAL JOURNAL OF FILM
AND VIDEO PRODUCTION TECHNIQUES
OCTOBER 1983
NEVER
AGAIN
HOW THE WEST WAS WON
THE BALLAD OF GREGORIO CORTEZ
THE GOLDEN SEAL

BERNIE DOWLING
MAN OF A
THOUSAND
FAILS
Film Noir Of Elisha Cook Jr.

John
Huston
AN OPEN BOOK
the autobiography

BY THE AUTHOR OF
THE SOUND AND THE FURY
SANCTUARY
WILLIAM
FAULKNER